"I wish I had r... ship role—it c... der-
Ruth Gral...
Father, For

"Every Christia... public servants, will benefit from the sound ... principles that are presented in this gold mine of wisdom."
Mike Johnson, Speaker of the US House of Representatives
Kelly Johnson, Licensed Pastoral Counselor

"Dave Wiedis offers safe and candid medicine for the heart of the servant leader. A good read and great gift for the called and chosen."
Dr. Alveda King, Speak for Life

"Pastors, scholars, Sunday school teachers, and Christians leading in the home will be challenged, encouraged, and enriched by this thoughtful, tender illumination of the throne room of the soul."
Dr. Peter A. Lillback, President, Westminster Theological Seminary, Philadelphia

"As both a professional counselor and pastor, I know the value of this self-examination both for ministry leaders and those they serve and highly recommend this book."
Winston T. Smith, Rector, St. Anne's Church Abington

"This book uncovers the hidden struggles of ministry, offering profound biblical wisdom and practical insight to help leaders overcome and find freedom from self-sabotage in Christ."
Tim Clinton, President and CEO, American Association of Christian Counselors

"With the compassionate heart of a wise biblical counselor, Wiedis addresses the very core of what drives people and controls their decision-making."
Shelby Abbott, Author; speaker; campus minister

"Dave has penned a thorough framework that holds promise for deep transformation and is very practical for becoming a spiritually healthy leader."
Paul Kuzma, Director and Board-Certified Pastoral Counselor, Center for Spiritual Renewal

"*The Spiritually Healthy Leader* is for all believers who desire to confront the ruling passions that keep their hearts from an uninhibited, authentic relationship with Jesus."
Jimmy Dodd, Founder, PastorServe; author

"In the *Spiritually Healthy Leader*, Dave Wiedis is the experienced counselor you need to enjoy greater freedom, loving relationships, and flourishing ministry."
Drs. Bill and Kristi Gaultiere, Founders, Soul Shepherding; authors of *Journey of the Soul*

"If taken seriously, this book will change you, then release you to be the leader you were meant to be."
Michael John Cusick, CEO, Restoring the Soul; author of *Sacred Attachment*

"*The Spiritually Healthy Leader* is a master work. I cannot believe how biblical, personable, and insightful it is."
Rick James, Founder, Cru Press; Publisher, Ratio Christi Press

"This book combines deep spiritual insights with practical steps to help Christian leaders in any capacity gain true freedom in Christ."
Michael Geer, President, Pennsylvania Family Institute, Harrisburg, PA

"Dave Wiedis provides real, workable tools and God-centered solutions to help leaders find freedom from self-sabotage. This will minister to many—pastors, counselors, mentors, and more."
Alan Sears, Founder, Alliance Defending Freedom

"Reading and digesting this book will save many pastors from self-sabotage and spare many churches and marriages from needless destruction."
Joe Watkins, Host, *State of Independence*, Lighthouse TV

"*The Spiritually Healthy Leader* provides an offramp from the Romans 7 hamster wheel."
Karl Benzio, Medical Director, American Association of Christian Counselors

"I am thrilled about Dave's new book, which is a must-read for anyone in church leadership or who aspires to be a ministry leader."
John Freeman, Founder, Harvest USA; author of *Hide or Seek*

"Dave Wiedis is a mature, kingdom leader whose impact has earned him a voice in the body of Christ. No one is better equipped to address the subject of healthy spiritual leadership."
Fred Hartley, Lead Pastor, One Mission Church; president, College of Prayer

"In *The Spiritually Healthy Leader*, Dave Wiedis helps us unearth and guard against the hidden drives that destroy a leader's effectiveness and legacy."
Dr. Chip Roper, Managing Partner, RKE Partners; president, the VOCA Center

"If you want to grow in your Christian walk and live a truly honest, healthy spiritual life, take the time to read this—it will change your life!"
Dr. Rhona L. Epstein, Author; speaker

"In a world of how-to books, this is an important exploration first and foremost of the root causes of spiritual health or unhealth."
Roy A. Yanke, Executive Director, PIR Ministries

"Providing biblical application to the discovery of our own ruling passions, Wiedis helps bring transformation to make Christ our ultimate passion."
> **Dr. Bruce A. McDowell,** President, Santiago Theological Seminary, Santiago, Dominican Republic

"With piercing honesty and profound wisdom, this book offers practical tools to address blind spots and ruling passions that can quietly sabotage leaders."
> **Matthew Maher,** Pastor, Landmark Church, NJ

"Dave Wiedis has walked alongside enough struggling pastors to be able to guide us to the heart of what we need—a heart open to the Spirit's transformation of our desires."
> **Rev. Dr. Sam A. Andreades,** Pastor; author

"This transformative guide ensures God's glory remains our driving passion. With transparency and grace, Dave models the freedom found in embracing our identity as those who are in Christ Jesus."
> **Dr. Kevin M. Flannery,** Senior Pastor, Church of the Saviour, Wayne, PA

"My congregation, our elders, and other leaders have been undone and then redone by the gospel wisdom found in this book. A great discipleship tool for heart transformation!"
> **Jonathan David Olsen,** Senior Pastor, Grace and Peace Community Church, Philadelphia, PA

"The principles outlined in this book have made a game-changing difference in my life and ministry."
> **Bruce Finn,** Former Coordinator of Church Planting, The Presbyterian Church in America, Philadelphia

"Dave Wiedis masterfully leads you to understand how ruling passions hinder your relationships with God, friends, and family, and he equips you to engage in an intimate, honest connection with the Lord."
> **Sue Corl,** Executive Director, Crown of Beauty International; author

"Dave Wiedis helped me see God's grace at work rescuing me from my familiar escapes and idolatries with insight, humility, and a heart for me as a pastor."
> **Andy Farmer,** Pastor; author

"With insight that can only come from decades of serving leaders, Dave takes readers on a journey through their hearts and ministers biblical truth to their worn-out souls."
> **Jeffrey W. Boettcher,** Lead Pastor, Christ Church South Philly; director of Planting and Partnership, Trinity Fellowship of Churches

"This book is a perfect blend of the tools necessary for leaders to have spiritual health and freedom in Christ while avoiding the traps we set for ourselves."
> **Sara R. Dormon,** Author; speaker

"There's a wealth of gospel-wisdom in these pages—for leaders and for all who follow Jesus."
> **Peter Nelson,** Senior Pastor, Goshen Baptist Church, West Chester, PA

"*The Spiritually Healthy Leader* is filled with Dave's knowledge to guide leaders toward healing and positive transformation."
> **Linda and Ken Koldenhoven,** Coauthors of *Connecting Around the Table*; cofounders, Creating For Him

"This is not just an insightful book—it's a practical, life-changing guide that will help you break free from bondage and step into greater freedom in your leadership and capacity to love."
> **Phillip Carnuccio,** Lead Pastor, Providence Church, West Chester, PA

"A must-read for any leader who wants to be spiritually successful following Jesus!"
> **Matthew Pieters,** Lead Pastor, BridgePoint Church, Valparaiso, IN

"Dave Wiedis teaches us how to root out our self-serving ruling passions and replace them with God-honoring worship."
> **Mark Hough,** CRU, People and Culture team, Southeast Region

"Filled with raw honesty and divine hope, this book is the spiritual and emotional equivalent of open-heart surgery. Pick it up and don't put it down!"
> **Rick Marshall,** PCA pastor; former crusade director for Billy Graham

"If you desire to better understand why you do the things you do and how you can live a transformed life, this is the book for you."
> **DJay Martin,** Pastor of Leadership and Vision, Parker Ford Church; lead editor of *Before the Booth*

"In Dave Wiedis's new book, he uncovers the nuances of the soul of man and gives practical advice for how to live above the traps of our flesh and the schemes of our enemy."
> **Jim Maxim,** Acts413 Ministries

"*The Spiritually Healthy Leader* is a GPS for hurting ministry leaders, guiding them out of the forest of failure, besetting sin, and misguided emotions."
> **Dr. Jeffrey S. Black,** Professor Emeritus, Department of Counseling and Psychology, Cairn University

"Dave transparently exposes the ruling passions and idols that derail leaders, offering gospel-centered tools to reorder their desires. Read it now—your integrity, calling, and leadership depend on it."
> **Dr. E. Scott Feather,** Lead Pastor, Gateway Church, Parkesburg, PA; author

"This book will lead you on a journey of identifying your passions, claiming their validity, and then aligning them before the face of God."
> **Patty Hutsko Brown,** Grace Church Bethlehem

THE SPIRITUALLY HEALTHY LEADER

FINDING FREEDOM FROM SELF-SABOTAGE

Dave Wiedis

New Growth Press
newgrowthpress.com

New Growth Press, Greensboro, NC 27401
newgrowthpress.com
Copyright © 2025 by Dave Wiedis

All rights reserved. No part of this publication may be reproduced, stored in a retrieval system, or transmitted in any form by any means, electronic, mechanical, photocopy, recording, or otherwise, without the prior permission of the publisher, except as provided by USA copyright law.

Unless otherwise indicated, all Scripture quotations are taken from the ESV® Bible (The Holy Bible, English Standard Version®). ESV® Text Edition: 2016. Copyright © 2001 by Crossway, a publishing ministry of Good News Publishers. The ESV® text has been reproduced in cooperation with and by permission of Good News Publishers. Used by permission. All rights reserved.

Scripture verses marked NASB are taken from the New American Standard Bible®, Copyright © 1960, 1971, 1977, 1995, 2020 by The Lockman Foundation. All rights reserved.

Scripture verses marked NKJV are taken from the New King James Version®. Copyright © 1982 by Thomas Nelson. Used by permission. All rights reserved.

Scripture verses marked NIV are taken from THE HOLY BIBLE, NEW INTERNATIONAL VERSION®, NIV® Copyright © 1973, 1978, 1984, 2011 by Biblica, Inc.® Used by permission. All rights reserved worldwide.

Scripture verses marked TLB are taken from The Living Bible copyright © 1971 by Tyndale House Foundation. Used by permission of Tyndale House Publishers Inc., Carol Stream, Illinois 60188. All rights reserved. The Living Bible, TLB, and the The Living Bible logo are registered trademarks of Tyndale House Publishers.

All emphases in Scripture references have been added by the author.

The names and identifying details of the vignettes and stories shared have been changed or presented in composite form in order to ensure the privacy of those with whom the author has worked. Three stories with identifying details have been shared with permission.

Cover Design: Faceout Books, faceoutstudio.com
Interior Typesetting and Ebook: Lisa Parnell, lparnellbookservices.com
Interior graphics: Shannon LoPresti

ISBN: 978-1-64507-499-1(paperback)
ISBN: 978-1-64507-501-1 (ebook)

Library of Congress Cataloging-in-Publication Data
Names: Wiedis, David, 1956– author.
Title: The spiritually healthy leader : finding freedom from self-sabotage / by David Wiedis.
Description: Greensboro, NC : New Growth Press, [2025]
Identifiers: LCCN 2024062178 (print) | LCCN 2024062179 (ebook) | ISBN 9781645074991 (paperback) | ISBN 9781645075011 (ebook)
Subjects: LCSH: Christian leadership. | Clergy—Psychology.
Classification: LCC BV652.1 .W483 2025 (print) | LCC BV652.1 (ebook) | DDC 253/.2—dc23/eng/20250121
LC record available at https://lccn.loc.gov/2024062178
LC ebook record available at https://lccn.loc.gov/2024062179

Printed in the United States of America

29 28 27 26 25   1 2 3 4 5

This is dedicated to my wife, Miho,
and my children, Kahn and Kiya.

Your honest reflections have taught me deeply about my ruling passions. You have lovingly reminded me that I am more deeply flawed than I believed and yet more loved than I could ever dare hope. I love you.

CONTENTS

INTRODUCTION   1

Part 1: The Problem

1. A VITAL MISDIAGNOSIS OF OUR SPIRITUAL HEALTH   10
2. WHERE PETER GOT IT WRONG AND WE CAN TOO: THE SUPREMACY OF RULING PASSIONS   17
3. WHEN GOOD GOALS GO BAD: THE ORIGIN, NATURE, AND FUNCTION OF RULING PASSIONS   32
4. RULING PASSIONS AND MOTIVES OF THE HEART   43
5. A PRELIMINARY DIVE INTO FINDING YOUR RULING PASSIONS   49

Part 2: The Consequences: The Destructive Nature of Ruling Passions

6. WE CAN'T SERVE TWO MASTERS   56
7. RULING PASSIONS WILL RULE OUR PULPIT AND SABOTAGE OUR MINISTRY   63

Part 3: Transformation: When Godly Goals Become Your Ruling Passions

8. CHRIST: OUR SUPREME RULING PASSION   78
9. THE SUPREMACY OF CHRIST AND OUR DESIRES   83
10. WHERE PAUL GOT IT RIGHT AND WE CAN TOO: THE SUPREMACY OF CHRIST   95

Part 4: A Biblical Response to Our Ruling Passions

11. PREPARING OUR HEARTS FOR TRANSFORMATION   106

12. ADDRESSING OUR RESISTANCES	118
13. IDENTIFY OUR RULING PASSIONS AND LET CONFESSION BE OUR RESET	123
14. ASK GOD TO REDEEM OUR PASSIONS	130
15. PROCESS EMOTIONS IN A GODLY AND HEALTHY WAY	141
16. LET CHRIST BE OUR STRENGTH	163
17. WALK IN THE TRUTH	169
18. A PERSONAL PLAN FOR TRANSFORMATION	187
19. PUTTING IT ALL TOGETHER: MY STORY	208
20. SO MUCH TO LOSE, EVERYTHING TO GAIN	222
APPENDIX: STORIES OF RULING PASSIONS	225
ACKNOWLEDGMENTS	237
NOTES	239

INTRODUCTION

My best friend, spiritual mentor, and pastor was killed instantly when he drove head-on into a beer truck while on a three-day crack cocaine binge. He was a gifted speaker and theologian, a highly effective teacher, and a respected preacher who exposited biblical truth with unusual clarity and winsomeness. He was a compassionate and skilled counselor. But it was not enough.

It wasn't enough either that he could compose music or skillfully conduct orchestras, or that he was a first-chair trumpet player. His musical gifts and athletic prowess were beyond what I consider fair for any one person to possess; he paralleled on his first ski trip, broke bricks as a white belt, and played competitive tennis and volleyball.

He did everything exceedingly well and yet it was never enough. It wasn't enough that his kids viewed him as a hero, or that his wife was a devoted spouse committed to working out their troubled marriage. When he abandoned his wife, family, and church, it wasn't enough to see the pain in their eyes or to hear the crushing disappointment and disillusionment of his congregation and friends who loved him. When his cocaine addiction became public, friends from all over the country reached out and offered to pay for rehab and to provide shelter and comfort. After he completed rehab, my wife and I invited him to live with us, incorporated him into our family, and tried to help him through his recovery. Our interventions saved him from a suicide attempt, helped him find a job, and provided a temporary safe place for his troubled mind to rest. That was not enough. The last time I saw him was immediately before he robbed us—while we were away on a family vacation. He went through our entire home and stole our money, valuables, family heirlooms, antiques, and my car, which was later found abandoned in a hotel parking lot in another state. A year later, he was gone.

Hundreds of people attended his funeral. The most common refrain was how this loving, talented pastor, mentor, and friend had such a positive influence in their lives. People testified about how he had led them to Christ and helped deepen their intimacy with God. They shared how his shepherd's heart had comforted them during their times of trouble and loss. His biblical teaching and his ability to listen, counsel, and love had profoundly changed their lives.

My friend's tragic death impacted me deeply. On a personal level, I experienced profound sadness. He influenced my spiritual and emotional life more than any one person on this earth. He was there for me during the most painful and significant events of my life, including my brother's death from a heroin overdose, the rejection I experienced during my heartbreaking divorce, and the rebellious and lonely years during which I had walked away from God to pursue serial monogamy. He listened compassionately to my deepest doubts and insecurities. His love for the truth and intellectual honesty inspired me to adopt

INTRODUCTION

those same traits for myself. He introduced me to and discipled me in the joyful truths of Reformed theology and helped reset my heart's affections toward God.

My friend's ministry illustrated the powerful impact of a pastor who is wholly submitted to the calling of the gospel and the eternal consequences of that good work. Ministry leaders are in one of the most strategic positions in the universe. They play a unique role in and have the potential to touch thousands—and in some cases millions—of people with the good news of Jesus Christ. Ministry leaders are on the front lines, preaching, teaching, and leading people to Christ. And they do more than preach the gospel—they help apply the gospel to every area of life so that everything they do has an eternal ripple effect on individuals, marriages, families, communities, and nations. Ministry leaders never know if the drug addict or business executive sitting in their pew, when transformed by Christ, will be the next Dietrich Bonhoeffer, Billy Graham, John Stott, Tim Keller, or Dallas Willard.

But deep spiritual transformation in the lives of others is severely jeopardized without the personal transformation of the leader's own heart. And it certainly does not take place if the leader is sabotaged by the idols of his heart. Ministry leaders don't usually implode from outside pressures but rather, the seeds of their destruction are already planted in their hearts, and they are incapacitated from within. As my thoughts returned to my friend's life and death, I was left wondering what events or factors initiated his tragic trajectory that ultimately caused this godly, gifted pastor to engage in such extreme conduct that destroyed his life, close relationships, and the ministry he sacrificed years to build.

In over three decades of experience as an attorney and in pastoral counseling, I have often worked with incredibly talented pastors who are admired for their godly character, dynamic leadership, and inspiring biblical sermons. Their congregations are impressed with their gifts, preaching, and powerful impact. Yet some of these same gifted leaders have destroyed their ministries and marriages through landmines of relational failure, financial impropriety, sexual immorality, narcissism, dictatorial leadership, or more subtle idols, illicitly fulfilling their longings for affirmation, admiration, control, or adventure.

How many times in the news today have we learned—as I learned about my friend—that a beloved pastor or prominent ministry leader has lost his or her ministry or marriage and brought pain and confusion to the body of Christ due to a misguided series of choices? Often, we are left in shock, shame, and fear. We wonder, *How did this happen?* How can leaders who have been called to ministry and are submitted to the lordship of Christ engage in such overt sinful conduct? What goes on in our hearts that can lead to actions that are antithetical to what we know to be true, and that offend the God we love so much? What lurks beneath the surface that has such power to destroy lives of such promise?

More personally, and more to the point—could this happen to me? To my life, ministry, and family? What goes on in my own heart that is contrary to the gospel, offensive to God, and harmful to myself and those closest to me? Why do I keep struggling with my sinful desires when I long to obey Christ and live a fruitful, loving, grace-giving life? How can I cultivate an "expulsive affection" for Christ that will transform my passions into a powerful, life-giving ministry?[1]

And even if a ministry leader is not formally disqualified from ministry, many leaders (and their congregants) who long for a passionate relationship with God can find themselves engaged in an endless cycle of shame and sinful, self-defeating behaviors despite their best intentions.

INTRODUCTION

We don't have to read far in Scripture to see that the Bible is replete with stories of godly men and women who, despite their intimate relationships with God and powerful public ministries, engaged in sinful conduct that wrecked their lives and ministries. David was known as a man after God's heart and yet he abused his power with Bathsheba, engaged in criminal conspiracy, and murdered her husband. Moses was the greatest Old Testament prophet but was denied entry into the promised land due to his anger. Jonah's bitterness and his demand that God implement his own version of justice undermined his ministry to Nineveh.

The premise of this book is that we are designed by God to be driven by a "ruling passion" to live wholeheartedly *coram Deo*, before the face of God. As will be further defined in chapter 1, a ruling passion is an extraordinarily strong desire that rules or controls us such that we make achieving that goal an ultimate priority.

Most Christians, and certainly ministry leaders, *claim* they have a ruling passion to have an intimate, obedient relationship with God and to be ruled by the lordship of Christ. However, there is often a great disparity between what we claim to be most passionate about and what our passions really are. Practically, we struggle in our relationships with others, battle with besetting sins, and are governed by ultimate motivations of the heart that conflict with Christ as Lord.

If you interviewed most ministry leaders and asked them the ultimate heart commitments that either motivated them to enter ministry or currently govern their ministry, you would likely hear statements like these:

- "I want to serve God with my whole life."
- "I want people to hear the gospel."

- "I want to help people know God."
- "I will go anywhere and do anything to share the gospel."
- "Obeying God is the most important part of my life, and I will teach others to do the same."
- "My ministry will be based solely on God's Word."
- "Evangelism is the most important endeavor."

In reality, these aspirational statements are often belied by actual—and often unconscious—ultimate heart commitments that are more accurately summarized by statements like these:

- "I will be liked."
- "I will be admired."
- "I will avoid pain."
- "I will be a peacekeeper."
- "I will be loved."
- "I will belong."
- "I will leave a legacy."
- "I will unify."
- "I will be unique."
- "I will be respected."
- "I will be in control."
- "I will have impact."
- "I will be the expert."

And this disparity, which grows in proportion to our failure to maintain spiritual and emotional health, can be devastating when lived out to its conclusion in our ministries, marriages, and relationships.

Ministry leaders must recognize the universal truth that anyone is vulnerable to self-sabotage when impure, self-protective heart commitments are adopted. The degree to which we are unaware of our ruling passions is the degree to which we will engage in idolatry of the heart. This book offers powerful strategies to help identify and understand how, when left unexamined, our ruling passions can serve as functional idols, permeate every aspect of our being, and have the potential to sabotage our relationships, ministry, and life. It is designed to help us identify our blind spots and learn how God can supercharge our ruling passions rather than letting them rule us—by bringing them under Christ's lordship to experience a radical, grace-filled transformation of our lives.

This book is an invitation to submit your entire being—including your passions—to the transforming work of God so that you will live every aspect of life in complete love for, in obedience to, and under the supremacy of Christ. It is an invitation to live coram Deo, before the face of God, so that your passions are transformed and your ruling desire will be to "love the Lord your God with all your heart and with all your soul and with all your strength and with all your mind, and your neighbor as yourself" (Luke 10:27). When practically lived out, the supremacy of Christ fills your mind, informs your priorities, and governs every aspect of your life and ministry. Then, we can live and walk vibrantly with God, free from self-sabotage of the heart; experience the ripple effect of health and healing in our own lives; and see that effect positively impact our close relationships, families, churches, and the next generation.

The principles in this book are not only for spiritual leaders, but they are also for all who desire to live in Christ. Every person in your church is governed by and will act in conformity with their ruling passions and may be potentially sabotaged by them. As a shepherd you have the special responsibility to lead and disciple them so that their hearts are yielded to the lordship of Christ. As you learn to identify your ruling passions, engage in the process of repentance, and experience deep heart transformation, you will be better equipped to powerfully minister to and shepherd the hearts of those in your church and ministry.

A CHALLENGE

What you read in this book may surprise and challenge you. You will see aspects of the gospel, yourself, and others that you may have never seen before. It is my hope that it will help you develop a deeper intimacy with God, a greater love for others, and a supercharged desire for—and submission to—the lordship of Christ in every area of life. But it takes honest, deep, prayerful reflection and a willingness to do the hard interior work necessary to deepen your walk with God. It is not easy. Everything within us tends to resist addressing the complicated recesses of our hearts. Consider this observation from Parker Palmer:

> That is why we externalize everything—it is far easier to deal with the exterior world. It is easier to spend your life manipulating an institution than dealing with your own soul. We make institutions sound complicated and hard and rigorous, but they are simplicity itself compared with our inner labyrinths.[2]

Are you ready to give up manipulating your external world and, with the help of God, enter the complex inner labyrinth of your own heart? Are you ready to rule the passions that want to rule you? I'm ready to join you on this journey. I promise that it will be worth it.

PART 1:
The Problem

Chapter 1
A VITAL MISDIAGNOSIS OF OUR SPIRITUAL HEALTH

How do you measure spiritual health? By what standards are we to determine the quality of our relationship with God? Christians tend to measure spiritual health in various ways: the length of their prayers, daily Bible reading, church attendance, spiritual gifts, a servant's heart, emotional maturity, or financial generosity.

Although these activities and traits may provide some *superficial* indicators of spiritual health, there is a far deeper, though less precise, way to assess spiritual health. To protect ourselves from a facile definition of spiritual health, we need a more robust framework. In 1677, the Puritan Henry Scougal captured the essence of spiritual health and expressed a way to "assess the beauty of an invisible heart." He said, "The worth and excellency of a soul is to be measured by the object of its love."[1] In other words, we can gain great insight into another's soul by what they are most passionate about, or as Scougal put it, the object of one's love.

What are you most passionate about? What motivates you and elicits the most energy from you? What are your ultimate commitments? Do you love people, history, music, art, and literature? Are you passionate about marriage and children? Do you focus your energy on cliff diving, exercise, collecting coins, shopping, gardening, or solitude?

Or perhaps your passions are different, less obvious, and potentially darker at their core. Do you find yourself obsessed with an inordinate desire for approval, affection, admiration, adventure, recognition, power, control, or impact?

Our passions reveal much about what we value, who we are, or, as Scougal put it, the "excellency" of our soul. Our answer to the question of what we are most passionate about will have an enormous impact on our life, marriage, and ministry—particularly as a ministry leader who wants to cultivate an intimate relationship with God. Frankly, our answer will put us on a trajectory to either living a life of faithful service to God or sabotaging our life and ministry. The spiritual health, wholeness, and "excellency" of our soul can be measured by who or what we love, where we spend our time and energy, what we dwell on, and what we most passionately pursue with all our might.

Our spiritual health is directly connected to our passions. Jesus said, "For where your treasure is, there your heart will be also" (Matthew 6:21). The first commandment tells us that God ought to be our first passion:

> "You shall have no other gods before me. You shall not make for yourself a carved image. . . . You shall not bow down to them or serve them, for I the Lord your God am a jealous God." (Exodus 20:3–5)

Jesus also taught that the greatest commandment is to "love the Lord your God with all your heart and with all your soul and with your mind and with all your strength" (Mark 12:30).

Accordingly, it stands to reason that our spiritual health can be measured by whether we pursue God with all our heart, soul, and mind, whether we love what God loves and pursue what God pursues. Our spiritual health can be measured by what we most prioritize—by what we are most committed to.

Take a poll of most groups of Christians today and ask them what they are most passionate about, and depending on their denomination or church "tribe," you will most likely hear an array of answers, such as

- correct theology
- the Word of God
- apologetics
- obeying God
- charismatic gifts
- spiritual experiences
- prophetic ministry
- justice, equality, and racial reconciliation
- evangelism
- worship
- church planting
- the body of Christ
- Christian education

While it may be true that they are passionate about these aspects of our faith, are these really the things about which they are *most* passionate? We may claim to be primarily passionate about God, but our moment-by-moment actions often reveal otherwise. Consider the following examples of gifted ministry leaders, all of whom claim a passionate love for Jesus and genuinely seek his lordship in their lives:

- Andy is an executive pastor and oversees a large staff. He always strives to make everyone feel accepted and comfortable and attempts to maintain peace with everyone. He avoids conflict at all costs. When loving confrontation is required, he shirks back in fear. Most recently, Andy ignored a key staff member's repeated poor performance, and the morale of the other staff is at an all-time low.
- Pastor John can teach well and pursues deep relationships. However, he has a propensity to be controlling. In the name of "accountability," he crosses boundaries by demanding access to the personal information of the other leaders in his church by requiring them to answer increasingly personal questions—even to the extent of asking to see their checkbooks or credit card statements and asking about intimate details of their sexual lives.
- As director of outreach, Mary strives to love others well. She seeks the deepest relationships with men; her female roommates report that she is antagonistic to them, underhanded, and impossible to live with. She needs to be the "queen," and when people show any attention to other females, she responds with a cutting anger that seems to come out of nowhere.
- Dan has been a respected elder for many years. He is fiscally responsible and has raised his three sons well. He finds himself uncontrollably drawn to public bathrooms seeking brief sexual encounters with other men. He acts out at least once a week, despite his desire for deep repentance.
- Nancy serves on the staff of a large church. She is artistic and loves serving others—until she inaccurately perceives others have abandoned her. She blows up at them

without any warning. Everyone around her walks on eggshells; they know her anger can go from zero to 100 in a millisecond.
- Jim is an evangelist who receives much adulation for his powerful and effective ministry. At home, he is a gentle tyrant. Everyone must focus on his needs. Even when he appears to move toward his wife and teenage children, he makes it all about himself, subtly manipulating them to affirm him. He becomes moody and petulant when he does not get affirmation. If anyone reflects his impact back to him, he appears to be oblivious and hurt.

These ministry leaders desire to live wholeheartedly for Christ. Still, they are ruled and sabotaged by functional idols that manifest as unconscious ultimate commitments that are contrary to Christ's lordship.

What are you most passionate about? How large is the disparity between what you *claim* to be most passionate about and what you are most passionate about *in practice*? We can claim to be committed to the gospel and at the same time have an ultimate commitment to getting relief from loneliness and seeking respite by engaging in sinful, destructive behaviors. We may claim to be committed to serving others and building a church that serves the community and at the same time have an ultimate commitment to impressing others or gaining affirmation. We may claim to be committed to working toward biblically defined social justice but at the same time have an ultimate commitment to maintaining power or control—of our ministries and others. The degree to which we are unconscious of our ultimate commitments is the degree to which they can control us and undermine our ministries. The premise of this book is that our spiritual health is measured by the object of our love which, in turn, is revealed by our *ruling passions*.

Ruling simply means controlling or governing. *Passion* is a powerful or compelling emotion or purpose, a strong affection for an object, person, or thing; it is something that we enthusiastically and intentionally pursue with great energy. As image bearers, we are driven by a strong purpose to pursue an end goal. A ruling passion is an extraordinarily strong desire that rules or controls us such that our energy is given over to pursuing and achieving this goal.

Sometimes, it is easy to identify our ruling passions. Desire to advance in our career, succeed in education, perform well in sports, and have a good marriage are obvious and clear passions. Desires for competence, affirmation, acceptance, control, and avoiding pain can be less obvious, subtler goals that can also rule our hearts. And it is quite possible to be completely oblivious to our goals because we can be unconscious and ignorant of the subtle motivations of our heart—those drivers that truly motivate us—at least until we hurt someone, or some unforeseen consequence of our ruling passion ricochets and smacks us in the face. Let me prove this by turning to a rich passage of Scripture that has some profound and surprising implications for us as we examine how the apostle Peter's ruling passion nearly sabotaged his ministry.

REFLECTION QUESTIONS

1. Henry Scougal said, "The worth and excellency of a soul is to be measured by the object of its love."[2] Do you agree with the premise that our spiritual health can be measured by what we are most passionate about? Why or why not?
2. How is this different from your standard for measuring spiritual health?

3. As you reflect on your life and ministry, what are some of the superficial standards you have used to gauge your spiritual health and the spiritual health of others?
4. If you have used superficial standards of measuring spiritual health, how may using such standards impede your spiritual growth and the spiritual growth of others?
5. Have you seen a disparity in your own life and ministry between what you *claim* you are most passionate about and what you are most passionate about *in practice*? Identify specific areas of this disparity.

Chapter 2

WHERE PETER GOT IT WRONG AND WE CAN TOO

The Supremacy of Ruling Passions

Paul's letter to the Galatian churches provides us with a great contrast between the spiritual health of two of the New Testament's most powerful and influential leaders, and it provides the theological foundation for our premise that our spiritual health can be measured by our ruling passions. In this chapter we will examine Peter's sinful ruling passion for self-protection and learn valuable lessons about the damage that results when ungodly passions rule us.

You can tell a lot about people by how they fight or handle conflict. Our conflicts reveal our character (or lack thereof), what we are passionate about, and the ultimate commitments that control our lives. In marriage counseling, *how* couples argue, attack each other, and defend themselves is often more revealing than *what* they are fighting about. A wise counselor observes the patterns of conflict, connection, and disconnection in addition to the content of the argument. The pattern of interaction can reveal heart issues.

In Galatians 2, Paul records a "fight" that reveals significant heart issues of both Peter and Paul, honestly portraying one of the most tense and risky confrontations recorded in the New Testament.[1] The conflict had the potential to not only rupture their personal relationship but also create the earliest and ugliest church split.

Significantly, both Paul and Peter had been captured by their passion for Jesus Christ. Both had been dramatically converted, Peter through Jesus's direct ministry on earth and Paul while on the road to Damascus. Both men had experienced dramatic heart transformation. Both were "apostles of Jesus Christ," specifically called, commissioned, and invested with authority by him. Both were honored in the churches for their leadership and had "been mightily used by God."[2] Both were engaged in dynamic, groundbreaking ministries as they preached the gospel, planted churches, and discipled new believers throughout the Middle East.

Peter's ministry focused on presenting the gospel to the Jews, while Paul's focus was preaching the gospel to the Gentiles. Both had apostolic authority and were entrusted with the "deposit" of God's Word (1 Timothy 6:20; 2 Timothy 1:14). However, this risky confrontation threatened to damage their relationship and split the church.

BACKGROUND TO THE CONFRONTATION

The Galatian churches had both Jewish believers and uncircumcised pagans who had been former idol worshippers. Although both groups placed their faith in Christ, they were from dramatically different cultures and had very different lifestyles, which created tension, offense, and conflict within the same church.

On the one hand, the Jewish believers practiced circumcision, engaged in ritual washings, and fastidiously observed Jewish dietary requirements. These Jewish believers kept to themselves, never interacting with or touching those they regarded as "unclean," lest they themselves would be defiled. To "an Orthodox Jew, sitting down to eat with pagans was an act of defiant rebellion."[3]

On the other hand, the Gentile believers did not have the same scruples. They would eat all foods, including meat that had been sacrificed to idols—an act that was highly offensive to their Jewish brothers and sisters. They viewed circumcision as a barbaric mutilation of the human body.

Phil Ryken notes that Antioch was the first church that had to address the conflictual dilemma of "table fellowship":

> Just as the Gentiles could behave as Gentiles, so the Jews could behave like Jews. But how was a Jew supposed to relate to a Gentile when they both worshipped in the same church? Did they have to eat together? . . . How could Jewish Christians keep kosher if they had to eat with Gentiles who ate the wrong food, prepared the wrong way, in some cases offered to the wrong gods?[4]

Although the Jews and Gentiles were fellow believers in Christ, there was a palpable tension between them. The Jewish believers were highly offended by the Gentiles' lifestyle and, therefore, refused to take communion or have any fellowship with them. As you can imagine, this split encouraged an air of arrogance, spiritual superiority, and shameless pride that gave even more grounds for personal and religious offenses.

Compounding this incredibly divisive environment was a false teaching by a small but powerful faction of Jews called the Judaizers who had infiltrated the Galatian churches. Paul characterizes them as "false brothers . . . who slipped in to spy out our freedom that we have in Christ Jesus, so that they might bring us into slavery" (Galatians 2:4). The Judaizers erroneously taught that faith in Christ alone was not sufficient for salvation. To become a Christian, one must first become a Jew, undergo circumcision, place faith in Christ, and maintain the Jewish dietary requirements (Acts 15:1).[5] They asserted that justification before God was achieved *both* by faith in Christ *and* by keeping the law.

The Judaizers' teaching directly conflicted with Paul's teaching that salvation was through faith in *Christ alone*. Convinced that the Judaizers' false doctrine was dangerous and antithetical to the truth of the gospel, Paul warns, "If anyone is preaching to you a gospel contrary to the one you received, let him be accursed" (Galatians 1:9). With an intended and possible humorous reference to circumcision, Paul states, "I could wish that those who trouble you would even cut themselves off!" (Galatians 5:12 NKJV). Given the tension between these Jewish and Gentile believers, the atmosphere in these churches was a religious and cultural powder keg.

THE DISASTROUS CONSEQUENCES OF PETER'S RULING PASSION

Against this tense and unpleasant backdrop, Paul confronts Peter, who had engaged in highly offensive, hypocritical behavior driven by his ruling passion. As you read Paul's description of his confrontation, ask yourself: What is Paul most passionate about? What is Peter most passionate about?

> Now when Peter had come to Antioch, I withstood him to his face, because he was to be blamed; for before certain

men came from James, he would eat with the Gentiles; but when they came, he withdrew and separated himself, fearing those who were of the circumcision. And the rest of the Jews also played the hypocrite with him, so that even Barnabas was carried away with their hypocrisy. But when I saw that they were not straightforward about the truth of the gospel, I said to Peter before them all, "If you, being a Jew, live in the manner of Gentiles and not as the Jews, why do you compel Gentiles to live as Jews? We who are Jews by nature . . . knowing that a man is not justified by the works of the law but by faith in Jesus Christ." (Galatians 2:11–16 NKJV)

What is so egregious about Peter's conduct that Paul feels compelled to publicly rebuke the *apostle* Peter? The enormity of Peter's sinful conduct here is often missed and worthy of explication. There are at least three offenses.

First, Peter's behavior created a "disastrous breach of fellowship" by greatly offending the Gentile believers over whom he had both apostolic and pastoral authority.[6] Prior to the arrival of the Judaizers, as an apostle and shepherd, Peter had engaged in regular and continuous fellowship with the Gentile believers; he had provided pastoral care, attended to their spiritual needs, shared communion with them, and treated them with dignity and respect.

However, when the men from James came, Peter withdrew and separated himself from the Gentile believers. Imagine what it would feel like if the apostle Peter had been your pastor, had provided you with loving and gentle pastoral care, had shared meals with you, and then suddenly shrank away in embarrassment, not wanting the Judaizers to know that he ever associated with you. One moment he is your caring shepherd and friend, and the next moment he backs away, acting as if your very presence taints and marks him as being unclean. For Paul, Peter's offensive behavior was harmful and inexcusable.

Second, Peter's actions influenced others to follow his offensive behavior, inspiring other Jews and Barnabas to imitate his conduct (Galatians 2:13). This further offended the Gentiles.

Third, and most dangerous, Peter's conduct supported the very heresy Paul is trying to correct. The Judaizers had claimed that Paul was an impostor because he had not lived with Christ, and that Paul's gospel of salvation through faith alone contradicted the additional requirements of keeping the law. Thus, Peter unwittingly gave the Judaizers both ammunition to criticize Paul as a false apostle as well as support for their heretical doctrine, undermining the truth of the gospel. Ultimately, Peter had believed the gospel but had failed to practice it. Indeed, Peter's conduct was consistent with one who *believed* the false teachings of the Judaizers.[7]

PETER'S RESUME DID NOT INSULATE HIM FROM SIN

Peter's conduct is even more shocking when one considers Peter's "spiritual resume." He was not a recent immature convert; he was an experienced apostle—hand-selected by Jesus! Considering the egregious impact of Peter's offensive behavior, we need to ask some really hard questions:

- Given Peter's high position and authority as an apostle, and his personal experience of living with Jesus, *why* did Peter commit such grievous sins against the Gentiles?
- What was going on in Peter's heart beneath his sinful conduct? What underlying issues were working inside him that would cause him to undermine the very gospel that he had given his life to preach?
- What was Peter's ruling passion?

Let's consider Peter's resume. Peter had left everything to follow Jesus. He had personally lived with him, eaten with him, and heard him teach every day for three years. John MacArthur notes, "Better than any other apostle, Peter should have known that in Christ all foods were clean and all believers equal. He had heard Jesus explain 'whatever goes into the man from the outside cannot defile him; because it does not go into his heart' (Mark 7:18–19)."[8]

Not just one of the twelve disciples, he was one of the *three* disciples closest to Jesus—along with James and John—and privy to more intimate time with Jesus than the others. Peter was an eyewitness when Jesus turned water into wine, healed the blind and deaf, delivered those afflicted with demons, raised the dead, and performed hundreds of other miracles. He was also present to see God honor Jesus on the Mount of Transfiguration, and he was in awe as Jesus spoke with Moses and Elijah (Matthew 17:2). And of all the disciples, Peter was first to identify Christ as Messiah, to which Jesus praised him, saying, "Blessed are you Simon Bar-Jonah! For flesh and blood has not revealed this to you, but my Father who is in heaven" (Matthew 16:17).

Peter touched Christ's resurrected body and was present at the ascension. He was present when the Holy Spirit fell on those in the upper room on the day of Pentecost. Peter courageously preached, and over three thousand people came to salvation (Acts 2). Given these spiritual bona fides, it's hard to imagine Peter sinning against his Gentile congregants so egregiously.

Perhaps we might be more sympathetic to Peter's sinful conduct when we consider his religious background and upbringing. He had the same religious and cultural background as the Judaizers, and therefore it is understandable that he would have had a natural tendency to identify more with the Jews than the Gentiles: he was a circumcised Jew, grew up in Jewish culture, and was conscientious about living a ceremonially clean life. However, years *before* Peter sinned against the Gentiles, he had received a dramatic vision from God, explicitly instructing him to never discriminate against the Gentiles and to treat them with the same respect and dignity as the Jews!

GOD'S REVELATION TO PETER

Acts 10 records an amazing revelation given to Peter regarding how he was to treat Gentile believers. Peter was visiting Simon in the city of Joppa. As he was on the housetop praying, he had a vision:

> [Peter] saw heaven opened and an object like a great sheet bound at the four corners, descending to him and let down to the earth. In it were all kinds of four-footed animals of the earth, wild beasts, creeping things, and birds of the air. And a voice came to him, "Rise, Peter; kill and eat." But Peter said, "Not so, Lord! For I have never eaten anything common or unclean." And a voice spoke to him again the second time, *"What God has cleansed you must not call common."* (Acts 10:11–15 NKJV)

Imagine how radical such a revelation would be to this Jewish fisherman who had been so completely steeped in Jewish tradition. To have kept himself separate from the Gentiles and then be told by God to now share the gospel with them must have been an incredible shock to Peter.

And yet, Peter responded humbly and obediently. Considering this radical revelation, Peter did the unthinkable to an Orthodox Jew: he accompanied Cornelius, a Gentile, to his home in Caesarea. There Peter explained precisely what God had revealed to him. "You know how unlawful it is for a Jewish man to keep company with or go to one of another nation. *But God has shown me that I should not call any man common or unclean*" (Acts 10:28 NKJV). Peter then presented the gospel, and the men were converted.

Peter's attitude and behavior toward people he had previously considered unclean immediately and dramatically changed. Instead of avoiding and despising Gentiles, he embraced them. In sum, Peter's intimate experience living with Jesus, God's explicit and radical revelation to him, and Peter's obedient, gracious response to the Gentiles made his later offensive behavior in the Antioch church even more puzzling and inexcusable.

PETER'S MOTIVES

The Scriptures make clear that God places a premium on the motivations of our hearts; there is great wisdom in looking beneath sinful conduct to examine our motives. When the prophet Samuel sought to anoint the next King of Israel, he was wrongly impressed by the outward appearance of David's brother. God instructs Samuel, "Do not look on his appearance or on the height of his stature, because I have rejected him. For the LORD sees not as man sees: man looks on the outward appearance, but the LORD looks on the heart" (1 Samuel 16:7). The writer of Hebrews states that the Word of God pierces through the externals and judges the "thoughts and intentions of the heart" (Hebrews 4:12).

What was Peter's motivation for his offensive conduct? Another way to ask this is, what was Peter's ruling passion? That is, what was Peter most passionate about as he ministered in the Galatian church? Paul explicitly tells us that Peter's motivation was fear and his goal was self-protection (Galatians 2:12). The Greek word Paul uses to describe Peter's "withdrawal" from the Gentiles is *hupostello*—a military term used for a "strategic military disengagement" to secure shelter and safety.[9] Thus, just as an army defeated in battle must retreat to seek safety and protection, Peter retreated in fear to seek his own safety.

The text does not state precisely what Peter feared from these men, but it is reasonable to infer that, at a minimum, Peter feared the criticism, ridicule, and ostracism that would result from the perception that he was unclean. After all, he was acting like a pagan in the eyes of the Judaizers and he likely feared that other Jews would be highly critical of him. Peter had previously encountered such a strong reaction from Jewish leaders in Jerusalem when they learned that he had delivered the gospel to the Gentiles (Acts 11:2–3).

Some commentators believe that Peter feared this group might report back to the leadership in Jerusalem that he had become defiled, and thus his leadership position would be compromised. Others suggest he was withdrawing due to timidity, fear of ridicule and peer pressure, or loss of popularity or prestige.[10]

Peter's behavior revealed that he was not a spiritually healthy leader. His ruling passion—his ultimate heart commitment, that which he was pursuing with the most energy at the moment—functioned as an idol of his heart. He was more committed to protecting himself than loving the Gentile believers or even obeying God. Peter's spiritual bona fides did not immunize him from a ruling passion for self-protection that fueled his overtly sinful behavior.

It is not that Peter did not love God; he was quite passionate about loving God and preaching the gospel to the Gentiles. But his ruling passion for self-protection at that moment stood "superior to any competing claim" that God had on his heart.[11] It was at odds with the vision God had given Peter to not discriminate; it led him to engage in behavior antithetical to loving others, it impeded his work of the gospel, and it nearly sabotaged his ministry. In service to his idol, Peter was willing to sacrifice his relationship with the Gentiles, the well-being of the church, the health and effectiveness of his leadership, and, ultimately, his obedience to God.

THE PATTERN OF PETER'S LIFE

In discerning our ruling passions, it is wise to reflect on whether there are prior patterns of the same behavior. Does Peter's ruling passion for self-protection remind you of any other events or patterns in his life? How likely is it that Peter had forgotten the dramatic vision or the amazing conversions of the Gentiles described in Acts 10? Did Peter knowingly and intentionally offend his Gentile brothers? Did he consciously desire to support the Judaizers' heresy? Did he consciously decide to disobey God's specific revelation?

It is doubtful that Peter was operating out of a conscious intent to sin or to hurt the precious people he was shepherding. I believe Peter was operating out of a ruling passion to protect himself—a heart motivation he had likely experienced over his lifetime but had failed to effectively address. As we look at other incidents in Peter's life, we will see that he gravitated to this core type of sin pattern in his life.

Remember that about twenty years before Peter exhibited this sinful behavior, he had another incident where he was governed by self-protection. Prior to Jesus's arrest, Peter had boldly proclaimed to Jesus, "Lord, I am ready to go with you both to prison and to death" (Luke 22:33). But within hours of this noble promise, Peter denied that he knew Christ on three separate occasions, even cursing to impress those around him with the sincerity of his denial (Matthew 26:69–75). Each time he denied Christ, Peter was motivated by fear and his ruling passion for self-protection. In other words, at that moment, his fear and self-protective behavior trumped his love for and commitment to Jesus.

Recall another time when fear ruled Peter. Peter and the disciples were sailing across the Sea of Galilee when a storm overtook them. Jesus walked on the water to be with them, and when Peter saw Jesus, he asked Jesus to command him to walk on the water too. Peter bravely stepped out of the boat into the water. However, as Peter walked on the water, he took his eyes off Jesus and began to sink. Matthew tells us, "But when he saw the wind, *he was afraid*, and beginning to sink he cried out, 'Lord, save me'" (Matthew 14:30). Interestingly, Peter experienced this fear *despite* the fact that (1) he had just observed Jesus perform miracles the day before by feeding five thousand people with a few scraps of bread and fish, (2) he had just witnessed Jesus walking on water, (3) Jesus was present with him, and (4) Jesus had commanded him to come out on the water (Matthew 14:28–33). Perhaps knowing Peter's ruling passion, Jesus had provided him with the opportunity to face it when Jesus was present with him.

Can you see the pattern of fear and self-protection in Peter's life? Although we cannot know with certainty whether earlier life experiences caused him to develop a vow to protect himself, it is reasonable to infer that he had repeatedly experienced fear in his life and, in response, had developed a ruling passion for pursuing self-protection.

Ruling passions, like other weaknesses, can lie unseen and dormant, but like an unseen landmine, they can explode at unexpected times. Peter's ruling passion for self-protection manifested itself on multiple occasions and created problems for Peter. During the long years between his denial of Christ in Jerusalem and his offending the Gentile believers in Antioch,

Peter failed to aggressively address his ruling passion of protecting himself. John Stott notes, "The same Peter who had denied his Lord for fear of a maidservant now denied Him again for the fear of the circumcision party."[12]

RULING PASSIONS DON'T ALWAYS CONTROL US

Ruling passions don't always define us; we don't always behave in accordance with them. Peter's life was not always defined by his ruling passion; it did not *always* control him. In the twenty years between the time when Peter denied Christ and when he offended the Gentile Christians, Peter intermittently experienced powerful transformations in his life and demonstrated remarkable bravery.

For example, Peter openly healed the beggar in public at the Temple Mount in Jerusalem (Acts 3:1–10). Then, with the beggar holding onto him, he boldly spoke the truth about the Jewish leaders' role in crucifying Jesus:

> "The God of Abraham, the God of Isaac, and the God of Jacob, the God of our fathers, glorified his servant Jesus, whom you delivered over and denied in the presence of Pilate, when he had decided to release him. *But you denied the Holy and Righteous One*, and asked for a murderer to be granted to you, and you killed the Author of life, whom God raised from the dead. To this we are witnesses." (Acts 3:13–15)

These are not the words of a man who was ruled by fear of others. Then, when Peter was hauled before the Sanhedrin and rebuked for preaching, the Sanhedrin was *astonished* by Peter's boldness:

> *When they saw the courage of Peter* and John and realized that they were unschooled, ordinary men, *they were astonished, and they took note that these men had been with Jesus.* (Acts 4:13 NIV)

After being told not to preach in the name of Jesus, Peter and John replied,

> "Whether it is right in the sight of God to listen to you more than to God, you judge. For we cannot but speak the things which we have seen and heard." (Acts 4:19–20 NKJV)

If Peter exhibited such bravery in these instances, how could he have exhibited such cowardice in Antioch? Ruling passions can lie dormant over time and become activated in periods of stress, anxiety, weakness, and vulnerability. When we are particularly susceptible, they can rise and sabotage our relationships or callings. Although your ruling passions may be out of your awareness and lying dormant, you have them. With God's help, you can discover them and be transformed so that you rule the passions that want to rule you. In our next chapter, we will explore the development and function of our ruling passions.

REFLECTION QUESTIONS

1. Read through Galatians 2:11–16. Assume the role of a Gentile believer in that church and discuss the impact of Peter's conduct. Can you give a similar example from the present day—in your life, your ministry, or other ministries—that had similar impact on you?

2. Peter's ruling passion for self-protection was motivated by fear. As you reflect on your life and ministry, identify specific events or issues that have caused you to experience anxiety or fear. What are some ways you have responded?
3. As you read about Peter's conduct, can you identify any analogous areas of your life or ministry where you have offended others by duplicitous or hypocritical conduct? How? Can you identify how that hurt or offended others?
4. Think about the courage it took for Paul to confront Peter. What kinds of doubts might Paul have wrestled with as he contemplated confronting Peter? Are there specific areas in your life and ministry where you need to confront others who are hurting those you lead? What concerns or fears do you have? How will you get the courage to address the issues?
5. After the revelation in Acts 10, Peter knew better than to discriminate against the Gentile believers. Are there areas of your life and ministry where you have known the right thing to do but failed to walk in it? Identify them.

Chapter 3

WHEN GOOD GOALS GO BAD
The Origin, Nature, and Function of Ruling Passions

We have defined a ruling passion as an extraordinarily strong desire that controls us such that our energy is given over to pursuing this goal above all other things. Admittedly, we don't normally think of things we are passionate about as negative; we usually think of being passionate about activities or things that give us pleasure, energy, or satisfaction. When I was growing up, I developed a passion for playing drums. I saved my money, bought my first drum set, and practiced for hours a day as my parents patiently endured the cacophony I created. I passionately pursued this interest and derived much pleasure in developing my drumming skills.

Like my passion for playing the drums, most of us have passions for many different activities and pursuits. Think about the following positive things we can be passionate about:

- professional success
- sports

- intellectual pursuits/education
- travel
- adventure
- music
- food
- marriage/family
- finance
- politics
- parenting
- career

Each of these passions can be healthy and good. Galileo is attributed to have said that "passion is the genesis of genius."

And yet, if our passions become ultimate pursuits and priorities in our lives and replace God, they can become functional idols of our hearts.[1] Timothy Keller has defined idolatry in a very helpful way:

> Anything can be an idol, and everything has been an idol. . . . [An idol is] anything more important to you than God, anything that absorbs your heart and imagination more than God, anything you seek to give you what only God can give. . . . An idol is whatever you look at and say, in your heart of hearts, "If I have that, then I'll feel my life has meaning, then I'll know I have value, then I'll feel significant and secure."[2]

Most understand idolatry with respect to material things such as wealth, businesses, cars, and homes, or sinful activities such as illicit sex, drugs, pornography, or gossip. However, Keller reflects,

> Sin isn't only doing bad things, it is more fundamentally making good things into ultimate things. Sin is building your life and meaning on anything, even a very good thing, more than on God. Whatever we build our life on will drive us and enslave us. Sin is primarily idolatry.[3]

The operating principle, then, is that I can take a good thing and make it an ultimate thing, thus making it an idol in my life. I am passionate about such diverse goals as ministry success, loving my family, counseling, skiing, hiking, bicycling, reading history, family genealogy, theology, and food—all good things. However, if I make any of the good things I am passionate about the ultimate goal that gives me ultimate satisfaction or meaning, they become more important than loving God, they will serve as idols in my life, and they will ultimately enslave me. The key questions then are these: What is ruling my heart in the moment? Is it an intimate relationship with Christ? A pursuit of the supremacy of Christ in my life? A hunger for the glory of God? A desire to obey him? Or something else?

Our hearts can be ruled by goals that can develop into a more subtle and insidious type of idolatry that can also lie hidden in plain sight. Here is an illustrative list of goals that we don't normally identify as idols but that can serve as the fuel for our ruling passions:

- affirmation, adoration, or approval
- security
- comfort
- being right or being the expert
- feeling good or pleasure
- power or control
- peacekeeping or avoiding conflict
- impact

- looking good
- avoiding pain
- never being vulnerable
- avoiding pain, abandonment, or rejection
- sexual satisfaction
- relational fulfillment
- adventure
- competence
- perfection
- love
- beauty

In their proper context and when rightly ordered, these longings and desires are normal, healthy, God-given, and congruent with being human. Jesus's explication of the Shema to "love the Lord your God with all your heart ... and your neighbor as yourself" (Luke 10:27) is not merely a command for us to obey; it is an expression of the deepest God-given longings for relationship with God and others that reside in the human heart. Most of us have healthy longings for relational connection, affirmation, love, peace, beauty, comfort, impact, and security. Most seek to avoid conflict, pain, and rejection. After all, who wants to be rejected, in conflict, or hurt? However, the desire to fulfill these longings can become sinful—functional idols of our hearts—when fulfilling them becomes a higher priority than loving and obeying God. When that happens, our devotion to them can become absolute. As Halbertal and Margalit explain, "What makes something into an absolute is that it is both overriding and demanding ... [and] claims to stand superior to any competing claim. . . . Any non-absolute value that is made absolute and demands to be the center of dedicated life is idolatry."[4] John Calvin observed that "the human heart is a perpetual idol factory."[5] When our hearts are ruled by an ultimate commitment to achieving any of the "good" goals listed above, the result can be even more insidious than those goals that are overtly sinful. Keller clarifies, "Anything can serve as a counterfeit god, especially the very best things in life."[6] When good goals to be affirmed, adored, in control, an expert, at peace, or free from pain become ultimate goals, they become sinful ruling passions that can have devastating consequences.

I once asked a friend of mine, Sue, why she had become a police officer. Her response stunned me. Without missing a beat, she described her horrendous experience with her abusive father. When Sue was around ten years old, he would periodically take her into the Everglades, place one bullet in his revolver, and force her to play Russian roulette. She calmly said, "I'll always be the one with the gun." Given her horrifying experiences, her commitment to "be the one with the gun" made perfect sense and led to her decision to enter law enforcement. In one sense, it was a good goal because it helped her function through such a difficult situation. However, being the one with the gun also served as a metaphor and organizing principle for how she related to her world. Her desperate need to be in control permeated virtually every other area of her life, career, and relationships. Imagine what it might be like to be Sue's husband, children, or colleagues. How might she behave toward them in situations that have nothing to do with guns and actual danger? What areas of her life would she need to control to provide herself with the emotional security that had been grossly violated by her father? Sue's ruling passion for control began as a good functional goal but turned into an ultimate commitment that became dysfunctional as it permeated every aspect of her life and ministry for decades into the future. To avoid being sabotaged by your ruling passion, it is imperative to identify your ruling passions.

IDENTIFYING OUR RULING PASSIONS

Ruling passions are core motivations of the heart that have their genesis in experiences and take the form of *vows*. I'm not referring to formal vows one might take in becoming a priest or admission into a formal organization, but rather expressions of the heart—decisions to live a certain way. For example, "I'll never trust anyone with my heart" is an internal vow that will deeply affect the person making that vow and everyone in a relationship with them. Therefore, a helpful way to begin to identify our ruling passions is to think about the vows we have made and why we made them.

Although most of us are not forced to play Russian roulette as Sue was, all of us have experiences that are painful or disappointing, particularly when our deepest longings are unfulfilled. In response, we consciously or unconsciously make internal commitments or vows about the way we will live life and how we will pursue what we are most passionate about. This makes sense because God is a volitional being who makes choices and moves with purpose. As image bearers, we too are volitional beings and are designed to make choices and move in directions as well.[7] When we make vows, we are exercising our volition to move with purpose to satisfy our longings for, among other things, relationships, love, affirmation, acceptance, security, creativity, and impact on others and our world. Our behavior will consistently reflect the motives and goals of our hearts (Mark 7:20–22).[8]

Our vows can be made at any time during our lives at any age and can be articulated simply and concisely. When they become ruling passions, they become the *organizing principles* around which we base our lives and engage our world. They become *sinful* ruling passions when our commitment to them is absolute. The words *always* or *never* usually attend to them and are clues that we have made a deep commitment that forms the basis of our ruling passions.

The following is a list of vows that are common to human experience. As you read through these, prayerfully ask God to help you identify any significant vows you have made and how they apply to your life.

- "I will never be hurt again."
- "I will never be rejected."
- "I will never be disappointed."
- "I will never disappoint others."
- "I will never be taken advantage of."
- "I will never be a burden."
- "I will never hurt others."
- "I will never be humiliated or embarrassed."
- "I will never trust another."
- "I will never appear to be weak."
- "I will never reveal my true feelings."
- "I will never be vulnerable."
- "I will never make others uncomfortable."
- "I will never be lonely."
- "I will make people like me."
- "I will always be successful."
- "I will be responsible."
- "I will get people to admire me."
- "I will seek the approval of others."
- "I will be loved."
- "I will avoid painful emotions in others."
- "I will avoid pain."

- "I will make people feel good."
- "I will have an impact."
- "I will be significant."
- "I will be in control."
- "I will be productive."
- "I will be busy."
- "I will always show my best side."
- "I will always know more."
- "I will be invisible."
- "I will be thin."
- "I will be important."
- "I will be seen."
- "I will be known."
- "I will only rely on myself."

As you reflect on this list, which, if any, stand out to you? Do any spark memories of past experiences? Perhaps a few of these apply to your heart. We often have more than one—"dueling passions"—that vie for our attention. There are many variations of these vows, so try to formulate your vow that reflects a core heart commitment that you have made.

THE ORIGIN, FUNCTION, AND PURPOSE OF VOWS

What compels us to make one or more vows and pursue them over others? Why does one person primarily pursue security while another avoids rejection? How do vows function for us and what purpose do they serve? How will they impact us in the future?

Our vows reveal longings that reside deep in our souls. These longings point to the way God has wired us to worship and find satisfaction in him.[9] But without the proper awareness that our longings point to God, the desire to fulfill them can be the seedbed for idolatry.

Our vows serve multiple functions. As with my friend Sue, they primarily protect us from pain or can be a strategy by which we derive safety, comfort, or even pleasure. Their impact is profound because, as ruling passions, they form the heart motivations that control how we live and engage in our world, relate to people, and make significant decisions. If I vow never to experience rejection, feel embarrassment, or appear foolish, I will organize my world in a way that protects me from the risk of those experiences. I will put great effort into managing my image by subtly crafting my appearance, presentation, words, and actions so as not to be rejected. I may hide my opinions in the service of avoiding rejection and looking good.

Don't underestimate the power of our vows; they have a profound effect on how we live and can set the trajectory of our lives. A young boy who grows up with dominating older siblings and feels the sting of sharp criticism may make a vow such as "I will never put myself in situations where I can be criticized" or "I'll never be controlled by others." As a ruling passion, his vow will affect how he relates to his siblings, friends, and teachers, and it can become a priority throughout his entire life. It will likely affect his decisions to take risks, try new experiences, pursue a career, or get married.

The "class clown" feels the momentary excitement of making others laugh and relishes the smiles he produces. He may vow to engage humorously with others to achieve that excitement, or he may use it to keep others at a safe distance so no one can get emotionally close enough to really know him.

A pastor with whom I worked was seduced as an adolescent by an older married woman who showered him with attention. The pleasure and affirmation he felt through that formative experience made him feel so alive that he continued to seek similar powerful experiences through illicit romantic and sexual relationships throughout much of his adult life. His unconscious vow to derive his own perceived self-worth from illicit sexual pleasure and affirmation from women became a ruling passion that could be articulated as "I will always gain significance through sexual pleasure with a woman who affirms me." Sadly, he acted out on this during his pastorate and marriage. Before he became aware of this formative vow, he was mystified by this behavior that violated his core beliefs in fidelity to his spouse.

A vow I made illustrates how our ruling passions can be rooted in less dramatic experiences and good goals. When I was in third grade, I took my first real test. I remember the absolute pride I felt when the test was returned with "100" written on it, and the teacher complimented me in front of the entire class. The feeling was so powerful that even half a century later I remember exactly where I was sitting and the look on my teacher's face. I recall making my internal vow at that moment: "I'll always study hard and get a perfect score on all my tests." Although I have faced the reality that getting a perfect score on all tests is not possible and is not necessarily the best measurement of my performance, this vow shaped the attitude I had in striving to achieve academic excellence.

Whether positive or negative, painful or pleasurable, each of us has had experiences that shape our vows, and those vows will powerfully impact our lives and ministries. As you continue reading, start to reflect on your vows and experiences. Be as specific as you can. In chapter 5, you will have a preliminary opportunity to identify your ruling passions and explore why they developed. Chapter 18 provides you with a personal plan for transformation where you will be able to do a deep dive into your ruling passions and place them in the context of your whole life's story.

REFLECTION QUESTIONS

1. Tim Keller observed that "An idol is whatever you look at and say, in your heart of hearts, 'If I have that, then I'll feel my life has meaning, then I'll know I have value, then I'll feel significant and secure.'"[10] As you reflect on your life, have you ever derived your meaning, value, significance, or security from a person, event, experience, or thing? Identify as many as you can.
2. The term *ruling passion* is defined as the ultimate commitment in our hearts that we most pursue with energy and purpose in the moment. Can you give some examples of things you most pursue with energy and purpose (e.g., food, pleasure, good reputation, control, peace, conflict)? Be specific.
3. Prayerfully review the list of vows on pages 38–39. Identify all that stand out and may be applicable to you. You may identify more than one or may consider vows that are not on the list.
4. Vows primarily function to protect us from pain and can be a strategy by which we derive safety, comfort, or pleasure. How would you describe how your vows function for you? What were you longing for when you made your vows?
5. Are you able to identify an experience in your life that caused you to make a vow? Explain.

Chapter 4
RULING PASSIONS AND MOTIVES OF THE HEART

To identify and understand our ruling passions, it is essential to have a biblical view of the motivations of our hearts. A central truth that runs throughout the entire Bible is that God cares deeply about our motives—why we do what we do.

> "For the LORD searches all hearts and understands all the intent of the thoughts." (1 Chronicles 28:9 NKJV)

> All the ways of a person are clean in his own sight,
> But the LORD examines the motives. (Proverbs 16:2 NASB)

> For the word of God is living and active, sharper than any two-edged sword, piercing to the division of soul and of spirit . . . discerning the thoughts and intentions of the heart. (Hebrews 4:12)

Jesus placed great value in the purity of our motives when he warned us to beware of practicing our "righteousness before other people in *order to be seen by them*" (Matthew 6:1). Jesus identified impure motives as the major flaw in the Pharisees; they demonstrated that it is possible to externally conform to standards that look good on the outside but still have impure motives. Although the Pharisees were intimately familiar with Scripture, memorized large portions of the law, and had outward demonstrations of righteousness, Jesus states, "These people draw near to Me with their mouth . . . but their heart is far from Me" (Matthew 15:8 NKJV). These religious leaders were supposed to be honest, transparent truth bearers, called to love God and others. However, the very qualities they were called to have eluded them because they failed to understand how their sinful motives undermined their relationship with God and harmed those they were supposed to shepherd. Like whitewashed tombs, they looked good on the outside but were "full of dead people's bones" on the inside (Matthew 23:27).

As you delve into identifying your ruling passions, you must be willing to cultivate a sensitivity to the complex motivations of your heart. Proverbs 20:5 states, "The purpose in a man's heart is like deep water, but a man of understanding will draw it out." Just as the bottom of a murky lake is hidden from view, our longings and motivations can be hidden from us. Likewise, our ruling passions can be very subtle and often lie below the surface of our awareness. This is why it is possible to go through one's entire life without a clear understanding of what they are or how they operate.

Because we are made in the image of God, who does everything with purpose, we, too, have a motive for everything we do—even if we are not aware of it. Think about your motivation for reading this book. You made a choice to read it, and your decision was not random. Perhaps you were intrigued by the title; perhaps you attended my seminar on this topic and want to learn more; perhaps you are bored and are trying to entertain yourself; or perhaps you picked this up off a shelf, only mildly interested in what it might say. Whatever your motivation, or whether you are aware of it, you had a reason for reading this book.

Sometimes we know exactly why we do what we do. When I'm hungry, I eat to satisfy my hunger. However, what about the times I find myself eating when I'm not hungry? I tend to use food as a surrogate for something else. I often habitually open the refrigerator, almost unconsciously, not because I'm hungry, but because I'm tired, frustrated, lonely, bored, or trying to satisfy some unknown internal angst. It takes awareness of my emotions, motivations, and longings to discern what is driving me.

It is one thing to be aware that I'm eating because I'm bored. It's another to lie to myself about my motives and yet be driven by them anyway. Sometimes I may find myself eating food and telling myself that I'm hungry when, in fact, I'm eating to satisfy some deeper need that food is not designed to satisfy. And sometimes we don't want to know what is going on deep inside of us because it is too painful. The Scriptures warn us that "the heart is deceitful above all things, and desperately wicked; who can know it?" (Jeremiah 17:9 NKJV). Because we are prone to self-deception and wanting to think the best of ourselves, we have a vested interest in not identifying motives that are "unacceptable" or hard to admit. Psychologist Diane Langberg reflects, "Self-deception functions as a narcotic in protecting us from seeing or feeling that which is painful to us."[1]

For example, it can be threatening to admit loneliness in marriage, not liking a lifelong friend, boredom with my job, or spiritual immaturity. When it is too painful or unacceptable to understand my own heart, it becomes easy to lie to myself and blind myself to what is really happening inside. Langberg also shares, "The more we practice [deception], the more we're able to do it without conscious thought," and that practice becomes habituated.² When we unconsciously and habitually engage in self-deception, hiding from what is true, we are setting ourselves up for the most extreme and dangerous form of unawareness, and we will chronically remain ignorant of our own motives. If we're going to walk with pure hearts before God and others, it's important to come to grips with our tendency toward self-deception and blindness.

THE ICEBERG METAPHOR

A helpful metaphor for understanding our hearts and the way we function is the metaphor of an iceberg.³ As it floats in the water, about 10 percent of the iceberg is above the water line. It is visible and can be seen by those around it. About 90 percent of the iceberg is submerged below the water line and invisible.

Imagine that what is visible above the waterline represents your external behavior, conscious thoughts, and feelings. This includes your motivations, goals, desires, and decisions. The part of the iceberg below the waterline represents those parts of yourself of which you are unaware, hidden from your consciousness. Included below the waterline are our motivations, our longings, and memories of past events that caused pain, guilt, or shame, as well as some of the impulses and desires of which we are ashamed.⁴ Most of us spend our time managing that which is above the waterline. The Christian world places great emphasis on the externals: how we look and behave, what we consciously think about, and how we manage our conduct. If we have a problem with lust, pornography, or anger, we try to manage the problem behaviorally; we are told to "stop it," or to read the Bible and pray, or to "obey God." There is a tendency to categorize bad behavior as "sin" and to think that we need to "repent" by exercising our will to control our bad behavior.

It is certainly true that we are sinful and ought to engage in repentance when appropriate, and yet it is also true that an emphasis on behavior management alone does not produce a deep change in one's heart. Merely focusing on behavioral change rather than God's transformation of our motives can turn us into frustrated hypocrites or judgmental Pharisees repeatedly bumping up against the same struggles throughout our lives with very little freedom. Very few people understand the complexity of the human heart. Jesus understood this complexity when he said,

> "What comes out of a person is what defiles him. For from within, out of the heart of man, come evil thoughts, sexual immorality, theft, murder, adultery, coveting, wickedness deceit, sensuality, envy, slander, pride, foolishness." (Mark 7:20–22)

If what is below the waterline represents our hearts, and as Jesus said, the heart drives us, then we must seek to understand that our behavior is a direct manifestation of the condition of our hearts. We must be willing to take a close look at the motivations of our hearts, even when they are hidden and hard to accept. Developing an awareness of our answers to questions like "What do I long for?" "What's really going on inside me?" and "What's my motivation?" is vitally necessary if we are going to discover our ruling passions and allow God to transform us so that we become free of their control.

MIXED MOTIVATIONS

As we examine our motives, we will find that they can be mixed. Consider the possible mixed motivations of a pastor who loves to preach and teach from the pulpit. He might be compelled to preach by a deep conviction that God has called him to this while at the same time seeking affirmation for his fine speaking abilities to satisfy his deep insecurities. He might be attempting to convince himself of his own worth or to impress others because he feels so unimpressive in other areas of his life. Or it could be a combination of each of these motives.

As part of the transformation process, we must reflect deeply on the motives of our heart and the commitments or vows we have made to ourselves about the way we will live our life. The next chapter presents an opportunity to reflect on what we have learned so far and begin to apply it to your life.

REFLECTION QUESTIONS

1. To what extent are you conscious of or in touch with your longings and motives? Can you give an example of something you did or said for which you could not discern your motive?
2. Can you give an example where you did something that looked good on the outside, but your motivation was something other than what you presented (i.e., selfishly oriented)?
3. Can you give an example of where you have lied to yourself about your own motives? Why did you lie to yourself? What function did it serve? What were you trying to accomplish or avoid?
4. How can you cultivate an awareness of motives? What does God offer us to address our own impure motives?
5. Spend some time in prayer and quiet reflection and ask God to make you exquisitely sensitive to the motives of your heart.

Chapter 5
A PRELIMINARY DIVE INTO FINDING YOUR RULING PASSIONS

Before we examine in detail how our ruling passions can sabotage our lives, it is important for us to begin identifying our ruling passions and how they originated in our lives. Ascertaining your ruling passions now will help you to apply the principles in the remainder of this book to effectuate personal dramatic transformation. After reading the guidance and examples below, use the Personal Worksheet at the end of this chapter to identify your ruling passions and to understand why they arose. This is a preliminary step to identify your ruling passions. In chapter 18, you will find a more comprehensive list of questions to help you further understand your ruling passions as part of your life's narrative. Most people have one or two predominant ruling passions, which I affectionately refer to as "dueling passions." These may be ruling passions that are similar or relate to each other. For example, "I will never be embarrassed," "I will seek to impress others," and "I will always be affirmed" carry a consistent message about the priorities of the person holding them.

Here are four steps to quickly identify your ruling passions and to express them succinctly (also available in the Personal Worksheet at the back of this chapter):

First, try to identify a vow or commitment that you have made that still affects the way you live your life today. A more extensive list of examples of vows can be found in chapter 3 (pp. 38–39), but here are a few common vows: "I will never be hurt," "I will never be embarrassed," "I'll always be the strong one," "I will always be in control," "I will always be affirmed." If you are not conscious of ever making a vow, that is understandable—many of us functionally live according to our ultimate commitments without having verbalized them. You may find it helpful to look at your behavior to infer how you functionally live out of a specific commitment that you have made. For example, you may not have expressly said, "I will never be embarrassed," but may live your life in a way that avoids embarrassment at all costs.

Second, identify the situation or experience out of which that vow arose. Vows are made because of either painful or pleasurable experiences. What happened in your past to make this vow so important in your life?

Third, describe the emotional responses that you had to the experience you identified. Try to name your emotions: Did you feel pain? Shame? Anger? Emptiness? Loneliness? How intense was the feeling? Where in your body did you feel these emotions?

Finally, how does this vow play out in your life today? How does this vow play out in your relationships, activities, and ministry? What situations trigger the vow?

As you think through these questions, consider these brief examples from three different people: Karen, Jack, and Dan.

A PRELIMINARY DIVE INTO FINDING YOUR RULING PASSIONS

You may find it helpful to read my story in chapter 19 to see how I identified and addressed my ruling passions and the larger context of how they impacted my life.

1. **Karen**: I made the vow to "never be humiliated in front of others again." That vow arose from an experience I had in middle school when my history teacher asked me a series of questions on a chapter in the book that I had failed to read the night before. I remember feeling hot inside, and I turned bright red. When the teacher saw that I did not know the answers, he continued to ask me questions to make me a lesson for the class. Fellow students giggled as I floundered in front of them, struggling to answer.

I now serve on the staff of a large church as the director of adult education. As a result of this early experience, I avoid situations where I can be put on the spot. I tend to experience embarrassment in situations even where I know the answers in subject areas I have expertise in, or even when my husband asks me simple questions about the way I interacted with our kids. I can see now that I avoid situations where I'll be subject to being questioned or humiliated, even if I do know the answers.

2. **Jack**: My vow is that "I will never be a burden to others." I made this vow when I was eight years old. My father was experiencing a long depressive episode, and my mother was overwhelmed by having to care for me and my three younger brothers while she was holding down two jobs to make ends meet. One evening, I remember feeling lonely. I went over to my mom as she was sitting on the couch and asked her to comfort me. She burst into tears and angrily shouted, "I can't take this anymore. How am I supposed to comfort you? Who comforts me?" I felt confused and embarrassed. I remember feeling a wave of guilt wash over me for making her cry. I told myself in that moment that I would never ask her for anything again, and that "I would always be the strong one." This theme continues

to play out today in many situations, particularly as a pastor. I have a hard time asking for help, even when I need it. I tend to do ministry on my own and don't even ask my associate pastor to help with hospital visitation despite my schedule being completely overloaded. I have a hard time letting my wife know when I'm feeling needy or lonely. This interferes with our relationship because she rarely can see when I need her and then I feel more ignored and lonelier.

3. **Dan**: A vow I made many years ago and continue to live by is that "I'll always know the right answer." Academics has always been easy for me. When I was in high school, I received a lot of affirmation from my teacher and peers during discussion groups. I led the debate team to a state championship. When I got to seminary, I excelled in the seminar classes and was asked to speak at chapel. Friends always asked me my opinion on doctrinal issues. When I know the answer or can give them wisdom, I feel a warmth or "glow" inside me and a feeling of pride. Now, as I lead my church, there is always this internal pressure that I always must be right. I position myself in conversations to "be the expert." If someone else knows more than me, I feel insecure and small. To make matters worse, even when I don't know the answer, I'll try to appear as if I do. It's hard for me to admit my lack of knowledge. If I'm honest, I lack integrity in this area.

PERSONAL WORKSHEET
A Preliminary Exercise to Identify Your Ruling Passions

Answer the following questions to begin identifying your ruling passions:

1. Identify a vow or commitment that you have made that still affects the way you live your life today (e.g., "I will never be hurt," "I will never be embarrassed," "I will always be in control," "I will always seek affirmation").

2. Sometimes a vow is made because of either a painful or pleasurable experience in your life. What happened in your past to make this particular vow so important in your life? Tell that part of your story.

3. What emotional responses did you have to the experience you described above (e.g., pain, shame, anger, emptiness, loneliness)?

4. How does this vow play out in your life today? What situations trigger the vow? How does this vow play out in your ministry?

REFLECTION QUESTIONS

1. What was it like to try to remember past experiences that have influenced the vows you've made? What obstacles, if any, did you encounter as you tried to remember past experiences?
2. What emotions did you experience as you filled in questions 1–2 of the Personal Worksheet? Identify all the emotions you felt.
3. What was it like for you to articulate your ruling passion and the role that it has played in your life?
4. As you look back at the ruling passions you have developed, are there any choices that you made that you would like to change? How would your life be different if you had made a different choice? Are there any that you would not change? Why?

PART 2:
The Consequences: The Destructive Nature of Ruling Passions

Chapter 6
WE CAN'T SERVE TWO MASTERS

What is wrong with developing ruling passions that protect us from pain or provide pleasure if we don't sin? Why would such positive desires like being a peacemaker, getting good grades, serving others, being successful in ministry, helping people, finding adventure, or avoiding embarrassment necessarily conflict with obeying God and embracing Christ's supremacy over my life?

Jesus said, "No one can serve two masters" (Matthew 6:24). You can't fully serve God and make *your own* goals or agenda an *ultimate* priority at the same time. These two goals are mutually exclusive. Either God is the center of your life, with your *ultimate* commitment to experience the satisfying supremacy of Christ and walk under his lordship, or something or someone else will be at the center. Anyone who adopts a different commitment or an internal vow as an ultimate commitment effectively disqualifies themselves from fully serving and obeying God. If a pastor's ruling passion is to not be offensive or hurt others, he may not be willing to teach biblical doctrines that may be offensive to congregants. If a pastor's ruling passion is to keep peace in his congregation, he may fail to fulfill his responsibility to address issues that may appropriately cause more conflict.

Let me illustrate this by taking some common ruling passions and show how, when taken to their conclusion, they will interfere with fully loving, obeying, and serving God and others. As you read this list, I encourage you to prayerfully focus on those that speak to you personally. Ask God to show you which ones specifically apply to your life.

- You can't fully serve God and at the same time have an *ultimate commitment* to "look good" because then you can't be a "fool" for Christ (in the eyes of the world). *Sometimes God places us in situations where we are called to be fools for Christ* (1 Corinthians 1:27).
- You can't fully serve God and at the same time have an *ultimate commitment* to be "in control" because God is sovereign, and he is in control. *Sometimes he calls us to be in situations where we feel out of control and still trust him.*
- You can't fully serve God and at the same time have an *ultimate commitment* to never be sad because Christ grieved and wept. *Sometimes God allows us to be in situations where he calls us to grieve and weep* (Romans 12:15; John 11:35).
- You can't fully serve God and at the same time have an *ultimate commitment* to never be disappointed because Christ experienced deep disappointment. *Sometimes God places us in situations where he calls us to experience disappointment* (Matthew 26:36–45).
- You can't fully serve God and at the same time have an *ultimate commitment* to be admired or affirmed because he always calls us to give *him* glory. *Sometimes he puts us in situations where we do not receive admiration or affirmation for his name's sake* (1 Peter 2:12; Acts 26:4).

- You can't fully serve God and at the same time have an *ultimate commitment* to "be liked" or popular because Christ was hated. *Sometimes he calls us to be hated for his name* (Matthew 10:22).
- You can't fully serve God and at the same time have an *ultimate commitment* to never be embarrassed because Christ was humiliated and endured scorn. *Sometimes he calls us to be in situations where we will be humiliated for his name* (Acts 17:32; 19:34).
- You can't fully serve God and at the same time have an *ultimate commitment* to never be rejected because Christ was rejected. *Sometimes he calls us to be in situations where we will be rejected for his name* (Isaiah 53; John 16:3).
- You can't fully serve God and at the same time have an *ultimate commitment* to be honored because Christ came to serve in lowly places and was dishonored. *Sometimes God calls us to serve in lowly places and be dishonored* (John 13; Isaiah 53:3).
- You can't fully serve God and at the same time have an *ultimate commitment* to be safe, because Christ was physically beaten and died for us. *Sometimes, God calls us to serve him in dangerous situations that place us at risk* (Acts 14:19; 16:22; 2 Corinthians 11:24).
- You can't fully serve God and at the same time have an *ultimate commitment* to never be lonely because Christ was left alone when he desired the presence of his closest disciples. *Sometimes God calls us to serve him in lonely situations* (Matthew 26:36–45).
- You can't fully serve God and at the same time have an *ultimate commitment* to be strong because Christ was "weak" (in the eyes of the world). *Sometimes God calls us to be weak in reliance on him* (2 Corinthians 12:9–10).

- You can't fully serve God and at the same time have an *ultimate commitment* to having a "large" ministry because Christ's ministry was relatively small. *Sometimes, God calls us to have small ministries that only impact a few.*
- You can't fully serve God and at the same time have an *ultimate commitment* to having a "successful" ministry as defined by extrabiblical standards because Christ's ministry was not successful according to today's standards (using modern metrics like size, number, budget, youth and Sunday school programs, special music, etc.). *Sometimes God calls us to fail by these standards.*
- You can't fully serve God and at the same time have an *ultimate commitment* to having an "exciting" or "vibrant" ministry because the sole criterion for Christ's ministry was faithfulness to the Father's will, regardless of how stimulating it was. *Sometimes God calls us to be in situations where we are bored.*
- You can't fully serve God and at the same time have an *ultimate commitment* to be physically beautiful according to our cultural standards, because Christ was physically disfigured for our sake. *Sometimes God calls us to be disfigured as we faithfully serve him* (Isaiah 53).
- You can't fully serve God and at the same time have an *ultimate commitment* to be sexually fulfilled (in behavior or perceived identity) because Christ fully served God as an unmarried, single, chaste man. *Sometimes God calls us to experience deprivation, to not feel fulfilled, and yet to fully serve him* (Matthew 19:11–12).

Loving and serving God with our whole hearts means that we will make his will and priorities for our lives our will and priorities, and that we will say yes to him even when it is uncomfortable, dangerous, or when we want to say no. It also means laying down our lives for him. Sometimes it means literally dying for him. More often, in our culture, it means subordinating our own desires, preferences, longings, and ultimate commitments to God and his will for us. Jesus modeled this for us when he left heaven to be a true servant:

> Though [Jesus] was in the form of God, did not count equality with God a thing to be grasped, but emptied himself, by taking the form of a servant, being born in the likeness of men. And being found in human form, he humbled himself by becoming obedient to the point of death, even death on a cross. (Philippians 2:6–8)

This is what Paul had in mind when he instructs us to "Have this mind among yourselves, which is yours in Christ Jesus" (Philippians 2:5). This is the way we are to follow Christ. Being under his lordship means we acknowledge that he is in control, and we yield to his will. When we live yielded to him, in all circumstances, we live according to his will and not our own ruling passions. On a practical level, this means the following:

- Our ruling passion to look good yields to being willing to be a fool for Christ.
- Our ruling passion for control yields to recognizing God's sovereignty over all situations and circumstances.
- Our ruling passion to not be disappointed yields to being willing to experience disappointment and yet remaining faithful to God and others.
- Our ruling passion for affirmation from others yields to being satisfied in receiving affirmation from God's unfailing love for us.

- Our ruling passion for being liked, respected, or popular yields to a willingness to be dishonored and despised for his name.
- Our ruling passion to never be embarrassed yields to being willing to be a fool for Christ.
- Our ruling passion to avoid rejection yields to being willing to be rejected for him.
- Our ruling passion to never be lonely yields to a willingness to be lonely for the sake of God's kingdom.
- Our ruling passion for adventure and stimulation yields to a willingness to be in a mundane, boring ministry environment that calls for faithful labor.
- Our ruling passion for a large, successful, or vibrant ministry yields to being willing to serve in whatever church or situation he calls us even if we fail by extrabiblical standards.
- Our ruling passion for sexual fulfillment yields to being willing to feel deprivation or disappointment without it destroying us.

Unless we are fully submitted to and under the control of God, we will be under the control of something else. Conscious or unconscious vows turn into ruling passions that can easily control us. As Rebecca Manley Pippert stated, "Whatever controls us is our lord. The person who seeks power is controlled by power. The person who seeks acceptance is controlled by acceptance. We do not control ourselves. We are controlled by the lord of our lives."[1] Tim Keller has beautifully helped us understand that whatever we are controlled by is what we ultimately worship. He defines worship as the "act of ascribing ultimate value to something in a way that engages our entire being and transforms our entire lives."[2] Thus, when we place our ultimate value on something that seems as aspirational as ministry success or as benign as gaining others' approval or avoiding emotional pain, those priorities—those ruling passions—become the practical object we worship, which controls us and can ultimately enslave us.[3] That which enslaves us takes title to our heart and causes us to serve it, rather than God.

In our next section, we will examine why the ruling passions that arise from our vows can severely damage our relationship with God, our relationships with others, and our ministries.

REFLECTION QUESTIONS

1. Many associate idolatry of the heart with sinful behaviors. Have you ever thought about the behaviors identified on pages 57–59 (e.g., avoiding sadness, disappointment, embarrassment, being strong, having a vibrant ministry) as idolatrous? If not, how does that impact you now?
2. Reflect on the following assertion: "Either God is the center of your life, and your ultimate commitment is to walk under his lordship—or something or someone else will be. Anyone who adopts a different commitment or an internal vow as an *ultimate commitment* effectively disqualifies themselves from *fully* serving God." What comes to mind as you ponder the implications of this assertion? Do you think it is too extreme?
3. With which of the statements described on pages 57–59 do you most identify? Why? Are there any statements that you would add to this list?
4. List five of the most important values you have in your ministry. If any of these values became ruling passions, how would it negatively impact your ministry and the people you serve? Have any become ruling passions for you?

Chapter 7
RULING PASSIONS WILL RULE OUR PULPIT AND SABOTAGE OUR MINISTRY

Our ruling passions *will* "rule our pulpit"—meaning, they will dictate how we live, do ministry, and relate to our family, staff, elders, and congregants. They will strongly influence, if not control, virtually every aspect of our leadership, culture, values, schedule, programs, counseling, sermon preparation, administrative tasks, evangelism, spiritual disciplines, relationships, and even interpretation of Scripture and preaching. If our ruling passion is to be in control, we will relate to our staff and congregants in a controlling manner. If our ruling passion is to be a peacemaker, we will avoid conflict at all costs, even when confrontation is loving, appropriate, and required. If we have ruling passions to impress others, to not be lonely, to receive affirmation, or to gain a sense of significance, we will manipulate our congregants to respond in ways that correspond to our needs. Unless we know our ruling passions, we have great potential to sabotage our ministry and run the risk of hurting the very people over whom we exercise spiritual care.

This is particularly true in the multiple ministerial roles and services we provide, whether that's preaching, teaching, visitation, administration, or counseling, because they are situations where we risk harming others by abusing our power. The relationship between ministry leaders and their congregants carries "inherent spiritual authority," and our position creates a power differential.[1] Pastors, counselors and other leaders, are in positions of power; congregants are often vulnerable, in pain, in trouble, or seeking direction and guidance. We must be aware of our underlying motivations in everything we do. The less in touch we are with our motivations, the more potentially harmful we can be to our congregants, as we cannot assume we are not manipulative. And, because we have a great capacity to manipulate others, we have great potential to move people to relate to us in ways consistent with our ruling passions.[2]

The potential to manipulate and hurt others is especially evident when we serve as counselors. In every counseling session, the counselor faces numerous choices about interventions to implement in each moment: when to ask questions, what questions to ask, when to engage in self-disclosure, whether to pursue one topic or another, whether to go deeper into the details of the counselee's experience, whether to deepen an emotion—the choices are endless. The decisions we make will be based on our motives and whether we are aware of them. This is why the degree to which we are not in touch with our ruling passions is the degree to which we are *dangerous.*

If we have the need for admiration, we will unconsciously (or consciously) manipulate our counselees to admire us. If we feel the need to be liked, we may manipulate our clients to like us. If we act on such motives, we are violating the basic premise that ministry is about serving our counselees' needs and not our own. When this happens, we move from serving others to only serving ourselves. This makes us *more* dangerous because we can hurt others and not even know it. Thus, ignoring our ruling passions is to invite disaster for ourselves, our congregants and counselees.

Although dramatic, the following case studies illustrate how ruling passions develop, their pervasive nature, and the potential tragic outcomes that can occur when ruling passions remain undetected.

THE LEADER WHO LIED AND DESTROYED HIS MINISTRY

John was the kind and compassionate president of a nonprofit organization whose ministry gave away millions of dollars of goods each year. He was also in serious legal trouble, having been charged with about one hundred counts of criminal fraud and misrepresentation. He showed up in my office asking for counseling after being referred by his attorney. John told me his presenting problem: "I lie but I don't know I'm lying." This may sound like a strange statement. How can a person lie and not know he's lying?

John explained the background. He had been a first responder immediately after the World Trade Center had been destroyed by terrorists on 9/11. He volunteered to help with rescue efforts at ground zero. After working there a few months he then went on a national speaking tour to raise money for the families of those who lost their lives. John told me that when he watched a videotape of himself giving his testimony at a fundraising event, he heard himself blatantly lie when he said, "I helped minister in New York City after the 9/11 attack just like I helped out in Oklahoma City after the federal building had been bombed." I asked, "What was the lie?" John said, "Dave, I have never been to Oklahoma City in my life." He explained further, "I have no memory of saying those words when I was on stage, and if you had told me I had said these words, I would have called you a liar! But the tape does not lie! There I am, lying on the tape, and that's proof enough. What's wrong with me?"

Exploring John's personal history and the development of his ruling passions illuminated why he had become so deceptive, to the point of being a pathological liar. He described his father as a "tough Irish policeman" who had been extremely abusive. John had been chronically ill as a child and his father was ashamed of John's frail state and his failure to fight or defend himself when picked on by neighborhood boys. Instead of empathizing or offering to protect him, his father severely punished John by forcing him to dress up in girl's clothing and sit outside on the steps all day long, subject to the humiliating taunt of the other neighborhood boys. This intensely painful experience led John to make the following vows: "I will never be humiliated again. I will never put myself in a position where I will feel the embarrassment and shame I felt when I was teased by those boys." Feeling his father's shame and disapproval only fueled John's longing for his father's love and affection.

John also related that his parents showed greater interest and delight in him when he embellished stories of what he did in school, inventing details to make them more exciting. Receiving the admiration he craved led to other internal vows: "I will impress others. I will get others to admire me." Over the years, these vows became the foundation for developing a dishonest style of relating to people. After spending years in sales and marketing where his exaggerations became habitual, automatic, and unconscious, John created charitable ministries to serve needy communities. Although he never stole anything, he engaged in "puffing," exaggerated his abilities, made misrepresentations to donors and vendors, and commingled funds. He lied to himself, he lied about finances, and he lied about essential facts in ministry. John's life demonstrated that the "penalty of deception is to become a deception, with all sense of moral discrimination vitiated. A man who lies habitually becomes a lie, and it is increasingly impossible for him to know when he is lying and when he is not."[3] Virtually unaware of the degree to which self-deception had overtaken him, John viewed himself as serving the kingdom of God and helping others in desperate need. He loved the admiration he received; he often portrayed himself as "noble" and as the "hero." Looking back over his life, he observed how he saw himself: "I'm the knight in shining armor."

As we uncovered his history of abuse and pattern of lying, John was able to see that his understandable longing for admiration, love, and respect morphed into an ugly, sinful ruling passion that could be articulated like this: "I will get others to love and admire me no matter what, even if it means exaggerating, lying, and deceiving others." This led him to sin against the Lord and others. As a result, John's multimillion-dollar ministries imploded, he lost his friends and his marriage, and he ended up serving time in prison for fraud. Being able to get insight into the genesis of his ruling passions helped him to develop more awareness of what drove his behaviors and their impact and to ultimately engage in significant repentance.

THE PASTOR WHO FAILED TO PROVIDE PASTORAL CARE

Pastor Timothy was a good communicator and biblical expositor. He loved to study and preach but had difficulty initiating deep relationships and providing pastoral care. In his church, he initially appeared personable and charming but failed to follow through relationally. Over the years, congregants consistently complained about his lack of involvement in their lives. They would make comments such as "He is a great teacher, but he never calls," "I love his sermons, but I don't know him," and

"He shows up when he has to, but he never pursues any relationship with me—I have been a member for years, but he doesn't know me."

The pressure increased when his elders confronted him with an example of his pastoral neglect that hurt a young man—illustrating how Timothy's ruling passion "ruled his pulpit." This young man had sought pastoral counseling from Timothy and had bravely summoned the courage to reveal for the first time in his life that he had been sexually abused as a young child. Voicing this was incredibly difficult; the congregant had experienced much pain and shame because of his abuse. In the counseling session, Timothy responded empathetically, showing great concern. However, due to his tendency to remain uninvolved and distant, he failed to follow up or even ask his congregant how he was or whether he had found professional help. Timothy's lack of pastoral care deeply hurt this church member and caused him to leave the church.

When the elders addressed this issue with him, Timothy minimized the problem and blamed others. His self-deception made it too difficult to admit to himself that he did not *want* to pursue or be involved with his congregants on a personal level; this realization was too threatening to his false perception that he was an effective, caring pastor. He knew that an essential job requirement of pastoral ministry is providing pastoral care and that a good shepherd knows and cares deeply for his flock. This flaw was widely known to everyone—except Timothy, who remained self-deceived.

When I met with Timothy, we sought to discover the ruling passion underneath his behavior. For true change to occur, he needed to get to the heart of his ruling passions. Wishful thinking and good intentions were not enough. Unless we understand and change our vows, we will be ruled by them.

Timothy's natural tendency toward introversion did not explain his aversion to genuine relationships.

We started with his family background. As the oldest of seven younger siblings, his parents placed high demands on Timothy to be responsible for the primary care of his siblings and held him accountable for their problems. His father was a pastor and was not present; his mother was depressed and both emotionally and physically absent from the family. He often felt overwhelmed and like a failure for not being able to live up to the demands of his parents.

As we explored that formative time, he discovered that he had made a silent vow to himself: "Don't get involved; it's too overwhelming and I can't help anyway." He was unaware of this vow until we explored the impact of his inability to satisfy the demands of his parents. In addition to his difficult past, Timothy had two young children with special needs who demanded his attention, and his wife suffered from extended periods of depression, which made her unavailable to her family. Although he did his best to meet his family's needs, he found himself living out his ruling passion by "checking out" with video games, scrolling, and being emotionally unavailable to both his family and congregants. Thus, Timothy's unconscious vow to "not get involved" in what he perceived to be relationships that would feel "overwhelming" eviscerated his motivation to pursue meaningful relationships at church and made him ineffective in providing pastoral care to his congregants. As Timothy became more honest with himself, he identified and admitted his unconscious ruling passions and bravely addressed this pastoral weakness in a healthy way. His lack of desire to provide pastoral care, which had previously mystified him, began to make sense. He stopped wallowing in the shame of unacknowledged desires and took significant steps toward true change.

THE PASTOR WHO DEVELOPED AN ADDICTION

My best friend, who was described earlier in the introduction, was destroyed by his ruling passion for ministry success, which he defined as being the expert and being smarter, more knowledgeable, and more competent than anyone else. As a pastor, he developed an encyclopedic knowledge of theology and with his natural brilliance could out-argue and out-reason the best.

When I was practicing law, I would often invite him to come with me on my business trips to have planned time away from the pressures of ministry. When we embarked on a trip to Nebraska where I was giving a legal seminar at a nuclear plant, I did not know that Paul had developed a crack cocaine addiction. From the start he engaged in bizarre behavior. He showed up late to the airport gate, looking disheveled and tired. At our hotel, he seemed paranoid. He suspected me of looking through his suitcase, and he examined the smoke detector on the ceiling, looking for hidden cameras or microphones. He failed to pick me up as planned when I was finished teaching my seminar and vanished with my rental car for three days. When he finally showed up, he was hungry and filthy; the rental car was covered with dirt and corn stalks. He had driven the rental car all over Nebraska, fleeing from imaginary villains he believed were chasing him. He then admitted that he had begun taking crack cocaine a few weeks prior to our trip and had been suffering from paranoid delusions.

When we returned home, he resigned from his pastorate and I connected him with a counselor. The church he had planted shut down, leaving people hurt and confused. What drove this talented and gifted pastor to crack cocaine? Many factors contribute to this complex question. As we unpacked his story, he shared some pressures that motivated him to develop his ruling passion for perfection and "ministry success."

His father, a pastor, was a harsh, unpredictable, and unfair disciplinarian whom he could never please. His father had lived a duplicitous life and moved the family to a new pastorate in a new geographic region every few years to escape exposure. With each move, Paul attended a new school and had to prove himself to gain acceptance. He sought to impress people by being the best at whatever he tried and vowed to be the expert in everything he did.

His ruling passions for competence and excellence followed him into ministry where he created the self-imposed pressure of having to perform flawlessly, especially in counseling and teaching. But Paul could never live up to his own standards, and this caused deep shame. He viewed himself as being inferior and undesirable, which then heightened his deep longing to be seen as lovable, competent, and knowledgeable. Because of his perfectionist tendencies, he overscheduled himself throughout the week. Unable to maintain appropriate boundaries, he made himself available to many needy people to whom he ministered. He routinely stayed up until 3 a.m. the night before Sunday services to perfect his sermons. He acclimated to this frenzied schedule over years of ministry. The pressures of pastoral ministry, a series of painful personal relationships, and multiple conflicts in his church drove him to medicate his pain with crack cocaine. He told me, "I was addicted the first time I tried it."

Over the next year and a half, he tried to get sober. Despite wonderful support from his family and friends and two stays at in-patient rehabilitation facilities, he continued using. His wife and young sons bore the brunt of his addiction. He even lived with my family for a few months. The last time I saw him was immediately before he robbed us—while we were away on a family vacation. He pawned our valuables and stole our money and car. We never had the chance to reconcile. He was killed in a head-on collision while high on crack cocaine. Sadly, Paul's ruling passion ultimately led to the destruction of his ministry and church, hurt his family, and took his life.

BIBLICAL EXAMPLES

There is nothing new under the sun. The modern examples above are consistent with many tragic stories recorded in the Scriptures, as some of the best-known biblical characters also failed to be aware of and contend with their ruling passions. Consider the following brief observations about Moses, Eli, and David and the destructive nature of their ruling passions.

Moses

Moses was the greatest prophet and one of the most powerful leaders in the history of Israel. He bravely stood up to Pharaoh and led the nation of Israel out of Egypt. God revealed himself to Moses in the desert; Moses received the Ten Commandments and was known as a friend of God (Exodus 33:10–11).

Yet, it appears that Moses's ruling passion was his keen sense of justice, which fueled his overreactive, angry responses when he perceived instances of injustice. When Moses saw an Egyptian beating his Jewish brethren, Moses murdered the Egyptian and hid him in the sand (Exodus 2:11–12). When he came down from Mount Sinai carrying the tablets written by God and saw the Israelite's idolatry, his "anger burned hot, and he threw the tablets out of his hands and broke them at the foot of the mountain" (Exodus 32:19). Later, when God commanded Moses to tell the "rock . . . to yield its water," Moses's anger at the injustice of the rebellious Israelites caused him to disobey God by angrily and violently striking the rock

(Numbers 20:9–11). An internal sense of and love for justice is a good thing. When it became an ultimate commitment and caused an extreme reaction to injustice, it operated as a sinful ruling passion that sabotaged Moses's life and ministry. As a result of his anger and unbelief, God did not permit him to enter the promised land (Numbers 20:12).

Eli

Eli was a faithful priest and judge in Israel. He raised Samuel to be a powerful prophet. However, Eli refused to discipline his evil sons, Phinehas and Hophni. A devastating ruling passion is to "overprotect" our children from pain and disappointment, including failing to allow them to experience and learn from the consequences of their bad behavior. Protecting our children from pain is a good thing. When it becomes an ultimate commitment, it is a sinful ruling passion. We then tend to overprotect and over function for them, engage in denial regarding their lack of character, or, worse, fail to discipline appropriately. As a result of Eli's ruling passion, he and his sons met a violently tragic end (1 Samuel 4:17–18).

David

David was known as a man after God's heart, and yet he committed abuse of authority, sexual abuse, adultery, and murder. We may reasonably infer that his ruling passion at that time in his life was an entitlement to pleasure and power (see 2 Samuel 11:1). Pleasure and power can be good things. When they become ultimate, they operate as sinful ruling passions. Scripture tells us that David's behavior "displeased the LORD" (2 Samuel 11:27) and resulted in, among other things, the death of his child (2 Samuel 12:18). It is also noteworthy that, like Eli, David's failure to address the significant conflicts in his family and to discipline his sons had devastating consequences to his family, resulting in an attempted coup against David and damage to future generations of Israelites (2 Samuel 13; 1 Kings 1).

In the above examples, the modern-day and biblical ministry leaders genuinely desired to serve God and dedicated their lives and resources to him. They did not anticipate the tragic results encountered. In ministry, we are so absorbed in doing good works, serving others, and looking to glorify God that it is easy to look at our good intentions and ignore the areas where we are at particular risk. Yet the apostle Paul wisely admonishes us not to think of ourselves "more highly than [we] ought to think, but to think with sober judgment" (Romans 12:3). He further warns any of us "who thinks that he stands take heed lest he fall" (1 Corinthians 10:12). The tragic stories in this chapter call us to be sober-minded and illustrate a chilling but poignant truth. At a minimum, ruling passions can impede our relationships with God, family, friends, and ministry. At worst, they have the potential to take our lives. To avoid such consequences, we need to realize that we are all in desperate need of the transforming work of God in our lives and open our hearts to the ongoing sanctifying work of the Holy Spirit. In Part 3 we will explore how the supremacy of Christ in our lives is the foundation for transformation.

REFLECTION QUESTIONS

1. Consider the following statement: "You can't assume that you're not manipulative—you will try to get people to relate to you in a way that is consistent with your ruling passion." To what degree are you aware of your potential for manipulation? In what ways have you been manipulative? Can you give an example of where you have manipulated others in your relationships? Your ministry?

2. Consider how much training you have received about the inherent power of ministry leaders, and the power differential that exists between a leader and congregant or counselor and counselee. "The degree to which you are not in touch with the motivations of your heart is the degree to which you are dangerous." Can you give an example where you have seen this operate in someone's life? Where have you seen this operate in your own life?
3. What are the dangers of not being aware of the vows you have made?
4. Can you identify some of the ways that the vows you've made have affected those around you (spouse, children, friends, coworkers, the church)?
5. As you read about John's, Timothy's, and Paul's stories, can you see how the seeds of ruling passions can be rooted in early experiences of pain and pleasure? What lessons can you take away from their examples?

PART 3:
Transformation: When Godly Goals Become Your Ruling Passions

Chapter 8
CHRIST: OUR SUPREME RULING PASSION

Having examined how ruling passions can serve as idols of our hearts and sabotage our lives, let's examine what a ruling passion centered and focused wholly on God looks like. In answering this question, we will first turn to Christ as our model, and then consider the preeminence and supremacy of Christ. Then, in chapter 9, we will address the relationship between our desires and the supremacy of Christ. In chapter 10, we will look at how Paul's godly ruling passions governed his interactions with Peter.

As we have learned, we can be passionate about many things. Our dilemma is that we often make a good thing an ultimate thing, which becomes an idol. The profound answer to this dilemma is to look at how Jesus lived completely oriented to his Father. Jesus is the model for us.

Jesus was passionate about many things, but his *one ruling* passion was knowing the Father and doing what his Father called him to do—period. Consider that Jesus was passionate about an inexhaustible number of topics and pursued them wholeheartedly, including justice (Matthew 23:23), children

(Mark 10:13–16), healing the infirm (Matthew 15:30), anxiety (Matthew 6:25), relationship repair (Matthew 18:15), and the poor (Luke 4:18).

Although Jesus passionately pursued these "good things," they were not ultimate things. Although Jesus was passionate about healing the sick, he did not establish a hospital; although he was passionate about anxiety and depression, he did not establish a counseling ministry; although he was passionate about relationship repair, he did not establish a reconciliation or mediation ministry; although he was passionate about the poor, he did not establish a food bank. Nor did he establish a court system, law school, rehab center, retreat house, seminary, orphanage, and so forth. His ultimate ruling passion was to do precisely what God called him to do moment by moment as he lived out his ministry. That is our call as well. Every passion Jesus had was subordinated to and aligned with his Father's will. Jesus explained, "For I have come down from heaven, not to do my own will but the will of him who sent me" (John 6:38), that he only does "what he sees the Father doing" (John 5:19), and "I seek not my own will, but the will of him who sent me" (John 5:30). There are many great things for us to pursue passionately, and Jesus models perfectly how to do this. Admittedly, none of us have the same experiential connection to Jesus as he had to the Father. So how do we conceptualize, implement, and focus our lives as Jesus did with his Father? We must live entirely in alignment with the supremacy of Christ.

The *Westminster Larger Catechism* states that our "chief and highest end is to glorify God, and fully to enjoy him forever."[1] This summation of the ultimate goal in life is based squarely on the Word of God. In his letter to the Colossians, Paul explains that Jesus is the sine qua non of our existence: "For *by him* all things were created . . . all things were created *through him* and *for him*. . . . *in him* all things hold together. . . . that in everything he might be preeminent" (Colossians 1:16–18). The implications of these verses are as astounding as they are life-changing in relation to our ruling passions. When we read these verses, they most often bring to mind the incredible complexity and beauty of God's entire creation—from the expansive universe to the mountains, trees, and oceans down to the smallest atom. However, have you ever thought of *yourself*—your very being—as part of "all things"?

First, "*by* him all things were created" means that you and I were lovingly and intentionally created by God. Indeed, he "chose us in him before the foundation of the world" (Ephesians 1:4) and physically "knit" us together in the womb (Psalm 139). To realize that the God of the universe specifically chose us before the world existed and then uniquely formed us gives us inestimable value and informs the meaning of life and purpose of our existence.

Second, "all things," including you and I, were created "*for* him." We were created by God *for* God for his good pleasure and purpose (Ephesians 1:4–5). He takes great delight in who we are as his unique creation. And we will find the greatest purpose and fulfillment as we realize that we exist for him.

I catch a small glimpse of how God must have delighted when creating us for himself as I reflect on a gift I gave to my grandmother. She hinted that she would love to have a model ship I was building, and I decided to surprise her with it for her birthday. The model ship building process is detailed, arduous, and long, with thousands of small pieces to be carefully fit together. As I slowly built the ship over a few months, I was motivated to please her; my grandmother's delight was in my mind. Each time I carefully worked with the detailed pieces, painted a miniature figure, or rigged the sails, I thought of her. I imagined with great anticipation the future moment when I would surprise her with this exquisitely built gift. I intended for her to take great pleasure in and enjoy what I created for her. I built the ship *for* her. Though this comparison pales in relationship to the reality of God's loving motivation in creating us *for* himself, "all things" include me, my heart, my conduct, my relationships—my very being. *He* is the very reason for my existence. And God's delight in creating us for himself provides us with the motivation to love and please him in all that we do. The gospel is a transformative experience that ignites in our hearts a love for God designed to supersede all other loves.

Finally, you and I (like every atom of all creation) are literally held together by him. "In him we live and move and have our being" (Acts 17:28). In him "are hidden all the treasures of wisdom and knowledge" (Colossians 2:3). This underscores our absolute and utter dependence on him.

Given the supremacy of Christ over all things, he becomes the preeminent, ultimate passion of my life. With Jesus established as my *ultimate* priority, I will embrace *his* priorities, *his* teachings, *his* ways, and *his* will. My driving motivation is, as Jesus summed up the entire Law and the Prophets, to love God with all my heart, soul, and mind (Matthew 22:34–40). Loving God and others—and all that entails—is the ultimate ruling passion and glorifies God.

What this looks like in any given situation will depend on the circumstances, will require godly wisdom and discernment, and will require an openness and willingness to obey whatever God commands. When the supremacy of Christ is our ruling passion, we can pray, along with the psalmist,

> Whom have I in heaven but you? And earth has nothing I desire besides you. My flesh and my heart may fail, but God is the strength of my heart and my portion forever. (Psalm 73:25–26)

REFLECTION QUESTIONS

1. How do your views of the universe and everything in it change when you consider the preeminence and supremacy of Christ?
2. What happens to your heart when you consider that *you* were specifically created *by* God? Does your view of yourself and your value change? How?
3. What happens to your heart when you consider that *you* were created *for* God? How does that impact your view of your purpose and mission?
4. Reflect on Jesus's one mission being summed up in his statement "For I have come down from heaven, not to do my own will but the will of him who sent me" (John 6:38). How would your life and ministry change if you were able to live that out today? What activities (in life and ministry) would you stop? What activities would you begin?
5. Compose a prayer that expresses a heart fully surrendered to God and confesses the supremacy of Christ as your ruling passion.

Sample Prayer

> Lord, I give you full access to my heart and open it up to you. The desire of my heart is for the supremacy of Christ to be my ruling passion so that every area of my life is subject to you and under your lordship. I long to live in full obedience to your heart, will, and ways. I pray that my ruling passions for finding affirmation, significance, and identity apart from you will yield to seeking your pleasure and to doing all that you have called me to in both the big issues of life as well as the mundane.

Chapter 9
THE SUPREMACY OF CHRIST AND OUR DESIRES

If Christ is supreme in our lives, and we are living to grow in intimacy with Jesus and glorify God with our entire being, how should we view the desires of our hearts? When do our desires cross over into idolatry? How are we supposed to handle our strong desires for the things on this earth, such as good food and drink, material wealth, physical and emotional pleasure, or the legitimate longing for close relationships, affirmation, impact, success, competence, comfort, security, and love? Are these in competition with God or compatible with loving God? Should we never seek affirmation out of fear that our desires are too strong? Are we committing idolatry if we strongly desire to be successful, competent, or secure? Are we supposed to live in denial of the deepest longings of our hearts?

The wrong answer to these questions can lead to a Christian version of stoicism that can completely undermine the life of faith. As we will see, to not feel, to not love, to not desire, to not live and enjoy what the Lord has created would be to forfeit the original calling that God gave to Adam and Eve and gives to us today.

It is helpful to have a proper perspective on our longings. Many Christians tend to devalue longings, calling them sinful when they are not. Some err by being more permissive, thereby courting the danger of encouraging others to fulfill their longings at all costs, wrongly adopting our present cultural values that have made self-fulfillment the ultimate standard for achieving happiness. Many in our secular culture would shamelessly contend that our attractions or desires are the sources of truth and form the deepest aspects of our identity. We see this so acutely in our culture today in the areas of sexual and gender identity. If one feels a sexual desire for someone of the same sex, then that means they are gay. If one feels more comfortable looking or acting like what would be stereotypical or common for the other gender, or if one subjectively feels like a man living inside a woman's body or vice versa, then that means they are transgender. Issues of sexuality and gender dysphoria are complex and are not to be dismissed as a trivial displacement of desires, but the cultural dialogue around them displays the contemporary attitude toward appetite and desire that runs contrary to a biblical view of the purpose and meaning of desire.[1]

Eschewing these extremes, the origin and purpose of our longings should be viewed from a biblical perspective. Augustine believed that "God himself is the highest good, and that all other goods are lesser goods that flow from his hand, intended to lead us back to him."[2] We are created with longings for God, relationship, significance, impact, security, peace, beauty, creativity, happiness, love, and acceptance, to name but a few (see John 7:37–38; Psalm 42:1; Isaiah 55:1–3).[3] God has put eternity in our hearts (Ecclesiastes 3:11). Each of these longings speaks to a desire that resides deep in our souls and points to the way God has wired us to worship and find satisfaction in him.[4] This is consistent with the second part of the answer to the first question of the *Westminster Larger Catechism* which states that our chief and highest end is to *enjoy him forever*.[5]

So, one purpose of desire is to learn to love and enjoy God through the things he has made while realizing that *he* is the supreme good and that any lesser good will not satisfy our souls but will ultimately entrap and enslave us. Augustine realized this as he contemplated the exquisite nature of God himself in comparison to his creation:

> He who made all said . . . nothing will you find more precious, nothing will you find better, than Himself who made all things. Him seek . . . and in Him and from Him shall you have all things which He made. All things are precious, because all are beautiful; but what [is] more beautiful than He? Strong are they; but what [is] stronger than He? And nothing would He give you rather than Himself. If anything better you have found . . . you will do wrong to Him, and harm to yourself, by preferring to Him that which He made, when He would give to you Himself who made [all things].[6]

Thus, the creation and everything in it is made intrinsically beautiful by the one who created all things. We are to enjoy them as gifts from God and foreshadows of his character. To do this, and to avoid making these gifts into idols,

> We must trace the specific features of the things we enjoy back to their source in God. Created goods are temporal, finite streams that flow to us from the fountain of God's uncreated and unending goodness.[7]

C. S. Lewis observed that when we are focused on God our Creator as the true source of every "good . . . and perfect gift"

(James 1:17), everything in nature and every temporal experience is a "tiny theophany," a revelation that provides an occasion for the exquisite adoration of God, which causes us to be filled with overwhelming gratitude to our Creator. Such experiences should cause us to look to God as the source, just as one would see the sun as the source of a radiant sunbeam.[8] As we engage in the adoration of him who gives all things, "no pleasure would be too ordinary or too usual for such reception; from the first taste of the air when I look out of the window . . . down to one's soft slippers at bed-time."[9] Thus, when our longings are viewed from this biblical perspective, we recognize that the desires we feel here in this life are simply an echo of what we will one day experience in heaven.

> Creatures are not born with desires unless satisfaction for those desires exists. . . . If I find in myself a desire which no experience in this world can satisfy, the most probable explanation is that I was made for another world. . . . earthly pleasures were never meant to satisfy it, but *only to arouse it, to suggest the real thing.* . . . I must take care . . . never to despise, or be unthankful for, these earthly blessings . . . never to mistake them for the something else of which they are only a kind of copy. . . . I must keep alive in myself the desire for my true country, which I shall not find until after death.[10]

THE DILEMMA OF UNFULFILLED LONGINGS AND THE EMPTY SOUL

But what am I to do when I am still left with longings and desires that are not filled by God, or by any other thing? What should I do when, in my most honest moments, I admit that I desire and love the gift more than the Giver, the sunbeam more than the sun? The state of the human condition (and indeed, the reason idolatry occurs in the first place) is that we sinfully tend to make good things into ultimate things. The empty feeling is there by design because it points precisely to God and can never be fully satisfied in this life.[11] Even the empty feeling of homesickness is a deep "sacred yearning" that we need to "steward well" because it is an "ache for another time and place . . . the imprint of eternity within our souls."[12] But it is precisely that empty feeling, the feeling that "something has evaded us," that can cause us to double down and foolishly try to squeeze fulfillment out of the gifts that were never intended to fully satisfy.[13] Our misdirected and inordinate desires for these gifts, rather than the *giver* of the gifts, are like the foolish and futile behavior of the Israelites who abandoned the "fountain of living waters" seeking to quench their thirst from "broken cisterns that can hold no water" (Jeremiah 2:13).

We vainly try to drink from broken cisterns—sex, wealth, success, competency, affirmation. We then (1) blame ourselves for having these desires, (2) live under the false assumption that our desires are too strong, and (3) mistakenly believe that we must kill our desires. But as Lewis astutely observed,

> It would seem that our Lord finds our desires not too strong, but too weak. We are half-hearted creatures, fooling about with drink and sex and ambition when infinite joy is offered us, like an ignorant child who wants to go on making mud pies in a slum because he cannot imagine what is meant by the offer of a holiday at the sea. We are far too easily pleased.[14]

According to Augustine, the answer to our dilemma is to rightly reorder our longings and priorities so that one neither loves what he ought not to love, nor fails to love what he ought to love, nor loves that more which ought to be loved less, nor loves that equally which ought to be loved either less or more, nor loves that less or more which ought to be loved equally.[15]

Elaborating on this idea, Keller notes,

> Wise people simply do not accept their desires as they are, nor with hasty feet run to fulfill them. Rather, as Augustine counseled, they reorder their desires with the knowledge of the truth. The problem of the workaholic, for example, is not that we love work too much, but that we love God too little, relative to our career. What the righteous desire is ultimately God himself, seeing his face. "I . . . will see your face . . . I will be satisfied with seeing your likeness" (Psalm 17:5). Only if we cultivate our relationship to God and grow the desire for him will our other desires not entrap us.[16]

We must therefore not blame or kill our desires but rather "follow the sunbeam to the sun."[17] We are given gifts to enjoy by God. Our pets, a great meal, romance, sex, adventure, wonderful time spent with friends, the warm relationship with our spouses—all are gifts from God for us to enjoy immensely. Each is a gift that reflects the goodness of God and some aspect of his character. When rightly ordered, our affections for and enjoyment of these are to be followed back to God who "richly provides us with everything to enjoy" (1 Timothy 6:17).

WHEN OUR LONGINGS ARE RIGHTLY ORDERED

If our longings are rightly ordered, our ruling passion for the supremacy of Christ and intimacy with Jesus will help us prioritize the lordship of Christ in every area of our lives as Paul reveals in Colossians 1:16–20. At the same time, we will also recognize that we have legitimate longings for things like affirmation, impact, success, significance, control, and comfort. However, these longings will be subordinated to the *ultimate* goal of loving and obeying God—in whatever circumstances he allows and calls us to live. The result will be a heartfelt attitude that can be expressed like this: "I'll be whoever God calls me to be, and I'll do whatever God calls me to do, *even if* my longings are not fulfilled." This attitude of the heart can be illustrated by figure 1.

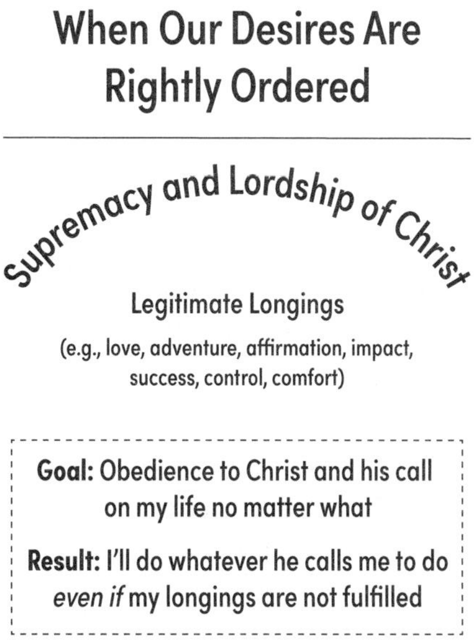

When Our Desires Are Rightly Ordered

Supremacy and Lordship of Christ

Legitimate Longings

(e.g., love, adventure, affirmation, impact, success, control, comfort)

Goal: Obedience to Christ and his call on my life no matter what

Result: I'll do whatever he calls me to do *even if* my longings are not fulfilled

Figure 1: Rightly Ordered Desires

This is consistent with Augustine's belief that "the *summum bonum*, the highest good, was God himself and that all other goods are lesser goods that flow from his hand, intended to lead us back to him."[18] When we walk in the Spirit and under the lordship of Christ, this subordination and submission of our desires does not suppress them and render them weaker, but instead *reengages* and *supercharges* our desires so I pursue that for which I was made, enjoy what God has created for us to enjoy more fully, and ultimately glorify God and enjoy him in them.

Consider how the outcome changes when the following ruling passions are rightly ordered:

- If my ruling passion is physical safety and God calls me to serve on the mission field in a dangerous location, I will obey God's call and subordinate my ruling passion for physical security, trusting my life to his providential care and control.
- If my ruling passion is avoiding emotional pain and I am in a painful marriage, I will trust God in his calling and subordinate my ruling passion to avoid pain and stay faithful to my calling to love my wife.
- If my ruling passion is seeking affirmation and I am called to spend time with and serve someone who never affirms me, makes me feel awkward, or is not pleasant to be with, I will subordinate my ruling passion by spending time with that person.
- If my ruling passion is comfort and my children need loving involvement, which entails engaging in activities that make me uncomfortable or anxious, I will subordinate my ruling passion to serve and love my children well.

When my longings are rightly ordered, *I will do whatever he calls me to do.* Augustine recognized the supreme joy that follows this heart attitude is a joy that is granted "to those only who worship you without looking for reward, because you yourself are their joy. This [alone] is the happy life . . . to rejoice in you, about you, and because of you. This . . . life of happiness . . . is not found anywhere else."[19] My experience has been that when my desires are rightly ordered and I obey him, I find the most fulfillment and joy.

WHEN OUR LONGINGS ARE NOT RIGHTLY ORDERED

When my longings are *not* rightly ordered, it may *appear* that I live by the supremacy of Christ, and I may claim that Christ is my priority, but in truth, my ultimate commitment will be to satisfy my ruling passions. They may be legitimate longings for things like affirmation, impact, success, significance, control, and comfort, but they will be pursued and prioritized over and above obedience to Christ. Then, my obedience will be conditional. Essentially, I will even end up *using* God to fulfill my own agenda. The result is an attitude expressed like this: "I'll do whatever God calls me to do, *only if* my longings are fulfilled." This attitude of the heart can be illustrated by figure 2.

When Our Desires Are Not Rightly Ordered

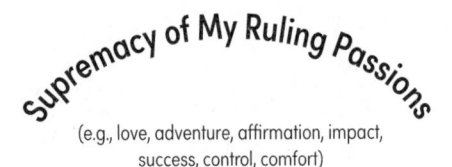

Supremacy of My Ruling Passions
(e.g., love, adventure, affirmation, impact, success, control, comfort)

Conditional Obedience to Christ

> **Goal:** Obedience to Christ *only if* my longings *are fulfilled*
>
> **Result:** I'll do whatever he calls me to do *provided that* my longings are fulfilled

Figure 2: Wrongly Ordered Desires

For example, assume three of my ruling passions are, as described above, my own physical safety, affirmation, and comfort, and I don't subordinate these to the lordship of Christ. On a practical level, I may resist or disobey God's call on my life to do dangerous missionary work; I will avoid spending time with people who don't affirm me or who make me feel uncomfortable; I will not go on a mission trip where I'll be physically inconvenienced and uncomfortable even when God calls me to do so. I may be more susceptible to having an extramarital affair with someone who will give me the affirmation that I desperately seek when it's absent in my marriage. When my longings are not rightly ordered, I will do whatever he calls me to do *provided that* my longings are fulfilled. My experience has been that when my desires are not rightly ordered I end up seeking to fulfill my longings by disobeying him and am left feeling profoundly empty.

Next, we will examine how Paul's ruling passion for Christ can be seen in some of the most well-known passages of Scripture he authored and then look more closely at how they played out in his relationship with Peter, who was ruled by his passion for self-protection. The preeminence of Christ as Paul's ruling passion is a model for us as we seek to glorify God and submit to the lordship of Jesus Christ in every area of life.

REFLECTION QUESTIONS

1. Take some time to prayerfully reflect on some of the deepest longings that you have. List them. What emotions do you feel as you get in touch with them?
2. As you reflect on what you most long for in life, how have you handled your disappointments when your longings remain unfulfilled? How have you dealt with the ache that stays in your soul even when some of your longings are completely fulfilled and they're still not enough?
3. Consider and identify specific areas in your life where you are tempted to engage in sinful behavior. What are you longing for? Can you identify the legitimate longing under the desire to engage in that sinful behavior? What emotions do you feel as you identify the longings under the longings?
4. How do you understand C. S. Lewis's assertion that "It would seem that our Lord finds our desires not too strong, but too weak"? Can you identify some of these desires in your life?
5. Which of the following statements do you identify with most?

"I'll be whoever God calls me to be, and I'll do whatever God calls me to do, *even if* my longings are not fulfilled."

"I will do whatever he calls me to do *as long as* my longings are fulfilled."

6. Can you identify a desire you have that could be supercharged and used for God's glory?

Chapter 10

WHERE PAUL GOT IT RIGHT AND WE CAN TOO
The Supremacy of Christ

In contrast to Peter's ruling passion for self-protection, as demonstrated by his treatment of the Gentile believers in Antioch, Paul's life exhibited his ruling passion for Christ's supremacy, which effectuated a dramatic conversion and transformation in Paul.

PAUL'S RULING PASSION FOR THE SUPREMACY OF CHRIST

Before his conversion, Paul had been a violent man consumed with a ruling passion to pursue his righteousness through the law, and by persecuting those errant Jews who had adopted what Paul considered to be a Jewish heresy, Christianity (Acts 7:54–58; 8:1; 9:1–2). As a devout Jew and Hebrew scholar, the seminal passage for Paul, as it was for every Jew, would have been inscribed indelibly in his memory: "You shall love the Lord your God with all your heart and with all your soul and with all your might" (Deuteronomy 6:5). In his religious zeal, Paul had erroneously assumed that the worship of Jesus was offensive to God and sought to eradicate the Christians. Paul was on the way to imprison Christians when he was converted on the road to Damascus and subsequently experienced a radical heart transformation (Acts 9). He went from being a "blasphemer, persecutor, and insolent" man to being filled with love for Christ and compassion for others (1 Timothy 1:13).

Later, when Paul was jailed for his faith, he expressed his ruling passion to honor and live for Jesus Christ for the glory of God and in service to his followers:

> It is my eager expectation and hope that I will not be at all ashamed, but that with full courage now as always Christ will be honored in my body, whether by life or by death. *For to me to live is Christ, and to die is gain.* If I am to live in the flesh, that means fruitful labor for me. Yet which I shall choose I cannot tell. I am hard pressed between the two. My desire is to depart and be with Christ, for that is far better. *But to remain in the flesh is more necessary on your account.* Convinced of this, I know that I will remain and continue with you all, for your progress and joy in the faith, so that in me you may have ample cause to glory in Christ Jesus. (Philippians 1:20–26)

By the transforming work of the Holy Spirit, Paul had repented and reoriented his ruling passion for righteousness toward the person of Jesus. He was now fully motivated by his desire to know Christ and to live in a way that accomplished God's purposes. His sinful ruling passion for pursuing righteousness through the law was completely transformed and properly reordered into his new ruling passion: the supremacy of Christ. He articulates this passionate desire in Philippians 3:8–11:

that I may gain Christ and be found in him, not having a righteousness of my own that comes from the law, but that which comes through faith in Christ, the righteousness from God that depends on faith—that I may know him and the power of his resurrection, and may share his sufferings, becoming like him in his death, that by any means possible I may attain the resurrection from the dead.

Paul's ruling passion for Christ is expressed in themes throughout the New Testament and demonstrated by his courageous and sacrificial life. This is specifically revealed in his letter to the Galatians, where Paul's ruling passion for Christ's supremacy resulted in a proper balancing of his passions for truth, the unity of the church, and Peter's spiritual health.

PAUL'S RULING PASSION FOR THE TRUTH

Paul is ruled by his passion for the truth of the gospel, having received revelation from God (Galatians 1:12), which he refers to as the "deposit" (1 Timothy 6:20). Paul exhorts Timothy, "By the Holy Spirit who dwells within us, guard the good deposit entrusted to you" (2 Timothy 1:14).

As evidence of his ruling passion for the truth of the gospel, Paul diligently battled against the influence of the Judaizers, expressing astonishment that the Galatians were "so quickly deserting . . . the grace of Christ and turning to a different gospel" (Galatians 1:6). Paul saw they were replacing the supremacy of Christ with a ruling passion for a works righteousness from which Paul had so strongly been transformed. He warns them:

> There are some who trouble you and want to distort the gospel of Christ. But even if we or an angel from heaven

should preach to you a gospel contrary to the one we preached to you, let him be accursed. (Galatians 1:7–8)

Regarding those who were "troubling" the Galatians, Paul states, "to them we did not yield in submission even for a moment, so that the *truth of the gospel* might be preserved for you" (Galatians 2:5).

PAUL'S RULING PASSION FOR THE UNITY OF THE CHURCH

Paul also had a ruling passion for the unity of the church. The Judaizers had infiltrated the Galatian churches; their false gospel created dissensions and divisions. Other divisions split churches in Corinth, Ephesus, and other places (1 Corinthians 1:10; Ephesians 4:1–3). His letters admonish Christians to maintain unity of faith in Christ:

> So if there is any encouragement in Christ, any comfort from love, any participation in the Spirit, any affection and sympathy, complete my joy by being of the same mind, having the same love, being in full accord and of one mind. Do nothing from selfish ambition or conceit, but in humility count others more significant than yourselves. Let each of you look not only to his own interests, but also to the interests of others. (Philippians 2:1–4)

PAUL'S RULING PASSIONS AND HIS RELATIONSHIP WITH PETER

Grounded in the ruling passion of the supremacy of Christ, Paul's life was reoriented and transformed in a way that was redemptive in others' lives. How did this play out in Paul's ministry to Peter? Paul's approach to those he ministered to was marked by a passionate desire to see Christ's character formed in them, so they too would live out of an identity found in Christ alone (Galatians 4:19). As one motivated to form godly character in Peter, Paul loves Peter enough to forcefully address Peter's destructive ruling passion "to his face" (Galatians 2:11).

Notice the following ways Paul lovingly confronted Peter. First, Paul accurately identified and named the problem: Peter was playing the hypocrite. Peter pretended to walk in love but was more concerned about protecting his reputation from the negative opinions of others. Peter had lived with and loved the Gentiles before the Judaizers came, but afterward he pretended to live as the Jews. Paul honestly reasons with him, "If you, though a Jew, live like a Gentile and not like a Jew, how can you force the Gentiles to live like Jews?" (Galatians 2:14).

Second, Paul subordinated his insecurities and desire for a "safe" relationship with Peter to love him well. What might Paul have felt like when he contemplated whether to confront the great apostle Peter? Paul had considered himself the "least of the apostles" (1 Corinthians 15:9), had murdered and imprisoned Christians, and had been accused of not being a "real apostle" since he had not lived with Jesus as Peter had.

In contrast, Peter's reputation and experience were formidable. He had spent years learning at Jesus's feet, performing miracles, and ministering effectively. Paul knew that Peter, James, and John were the apostolic "pillars" and had been the ones in positions of authority who had extended to Paul the "right hand of fellowship" (Galatians 2:9). Thus, Peter held one of the highest positions of respect and authority in the church. Paul had likely experienced some anxiety as he contemplated whether to confront Peter at all. Perhaps Paul was tempted to "let it go," cover it over, or at least confront Peter privately.

Thankfully, however, Paul was not awed by Peter's office, reputation, or experience to the point where he gave in to whatever feelings of insecurity or inadequacy he had. He stood for truth regardless of the prestige of the one who needed correction, and regardless of how uncomfortable he may have felt. Paul did not put his own feelings of relational safety first. He made himself vulnerable for the good of Peter and the church. The church desperately needs people of character who will place loving others and obedience to the truth above all else.

Suppose Paul had been conflict-avoidant and his ruling passion had been to keep the peace by making "false peace," to maintain his comfort level. If this had been his ruling passion, he would not have confronted Peter, which may have led to disastrous consequences for both Peter and the church.

Third, in relating to Peter as he did, Paul acted as a faithful friend. Paul did not allow Peter's offense to destroy their relationship or ministry. If Paul was still concerned with meriting his own righteousness, then this might have gone differently. And to Peter's credit, he was not offended and did not break off his relationship with Paul. A far too common response to a rebuke is to take offense and cut off the relationship. However, the mark of love is to work through conflicts and stay in the relationship even when it is difficult.

The Scriptures are replete with admonitions to correct each other to encourage spiritual growth (Hebrews 3:12–13). One proverb that has been particularly helpful to me in becoming less defensive about correction or critique says, "A rebuke goes deeper into a man of understanding than a hundred blows into a fool" (Proverbs 17:10). This has helped me embrace correction in my life. Peter's relationship with Paul illustrates this principle. Years after Paul confronted Peter, Peter affectionately referred to Paul as his "beloved" brother and referred to Paul's letters as the "Scriptures" (2 Peter 3:14–16). Thus, these two apostles' relationship benefited greatly from Paul's ruling passion for the supremacy of Christ, which led to a passion for truth and his courageous willingness to address Peter's sinful ruling passion of self-protection.

Finally, Paul's ruling passion for Christ and his righteousness, expressed in his desire to see Christ's character formed in Peter, played a significant role in Peter's repentance. This was evident when Peter testified before the Jerusalem council about the exact theological issue over which Paul had rebuked him. The Judaizers had been teaching that circumcision was necessary for salvation (Acts 15:1). At some point, Paul rebuked Peter before the Jerusalem council convened (Galatians 2:11–18).[1] Later, Paul and Barnabas were appointed to go to Jerusalem to address this issue, and there, Paul and Peter stood back-to-back, in unity on this issue. No longer controlled by his ruling passion, Peter made the following speech to the council:

> "Brothers, you know that in the early days God made a choice among you, that by my mouth the Gentiles should hear the word of the gospel and believe. And God, who knows the heart, bore witness to them, by giving them the Holy Spirit just as he did to us, and he made no distinction between us and them, having cleansed their hearts by faith. *Now, therefore, why are you putting God to the test by placing a yoke on the neck of the disciples that neither our fathers nor we have been able to bear? But we believe that we will be saved through the grace of the Lord Jesus, just as they will.*" (Acts 15:7–11)

A comparison of Peter's language in Acts 15:10–11 with Paul's rebuke of Peter in Galatians 2:16 reveals the influence Paul had on Peter. Peter's words mirror Paul's: "A person is not justified by works of the law but through faith in Jesus Christ . . . in order to be justified by faith in Christ and not by works of the law, because by works of the law, no one will be justified."[2]

In a situation that could have ruptured the church, this stinging rebuke instead brought about Peter's repentance and the maturing of his relationship with Paul. At the end of the day, both apostles glorify God by standing together in unity and in loving support of one another and the gospel.

That Peter's ruling passion for self-protection did not have the last word in his life is most clearly seen in the fact that Peter gave his life for the gospel. Indicating the way Peter would die, Jesus stated, "when you are old, you will stretch out your hands, and another will dress you and carry you where you do not want to go" (John 21:18). Between the time of Jesus's prediction and Peter's death, Peter struggled with the ruling passion for self-protection as seen in the way he hurt the Gentile believers. However, in the end, Peter repented; his ruling passion for the supremacy of Christ triumphed over his ruling passion for self-protection.

Having examined Christ's preeminence as Paul's ruling passion and applied it to the fruit this bore in Peter's life, we will now undertake the crucial task of responding biblically to the ruling passions of our hearts that have become idols.

REFLECTION QUESTIONS

1. How would you describe Paul's ruling passions before his conversion?
2. Think about Paul's dramatic conversion. What prerequisite knowledge and experiences must one have before one can even desire for Christ to be preeminent in one's life?
3. Notice that Paul had many good passions in his ministry (e.g., truth of the gospel, unity of the church, knowing the power of Christ), but his one main passion was for Christ to be preeminent. How do you reorder your many passions to make Christ your one ruling passion?

4. As you reflect on how Paul's ruling passion for the supremacy of Christ led him to address Peter with a firm, loving rebuke, how does that impact you?
5. In what situations have you been called or required to address weaknesses or sins in others? How have you responded? What fears or internal resistance did you experience? How did the other person react?

PART 4:
A Biblical Response to Our Ruling Passions

Chapter 11
PREPARING OUR HEARTS FOR TRANSFORMATION

As we turn to a biblical response to our ruling passions, let me encourage you to consider six ways we must prepare ours heart for transformation.

1. PRAY

First, it is imperative that we prayerfully embark on the process of repentance and transformation in God's presence, relying on his grace and the transforming power of the Holy Spirit to help change us gently, accurately, and skillfully. In other words, treat this transformation process as what it must be: a *grace-filled* transaction with the living God who *loves us* and is able to change us from the inside out. God is a God of grace. He looks at us through the grace-filled eyes of Jesus.[1] As you reflect on your life's story, which likely includes difficult experiences, your foibles and weaknesses, and your wounds and pain, try to see yourself as God sees you through the grace-filled eyes of Jesus: with care, love, and understanding.

The apostle John encouraged us with these words: "See what great love the Father has *lavished* on us, that we should be called children of God! And that is what we are!" (1 John 3:1 NIV). God speaks these beautiful words through the prophet Zephaniah: "The LORD your God is in your midst, a mighty one who will save; he will *rejoice over you* with gladness; he will *quiet you by his love*; he will *exult over you* with loud singing" (Zephaniah 3:17). Have you considered—or better yet, experienced—God lavishing his love on you, rejoicing over you with gladness, exulting over you with loud singing? The difference between intellectually understanding and experientially knowing God's love is profound; the latter helps us to repent and reorder our desires toward Christ so our ruling passions assume their rightful place before God.

We are wholly dependent on God and cannot be transformed without him. We can't give ourselves heart transplants; he can. Invite God to guide you through the process and give you the eyes to see things you have not previously seen in yourself, in your circumstances, and in God. And because engaging in this biblical process of responding to your ruling passions can be painful, allow him to comfort you and heal you of your wounds. One of the names of the Holy Spirit is *Paraclete*, meaning "the comforter" (John 14:16, 26 NKJV). Invite him to comfort you. Perhaps most important in this process of repentance, I encourage you to allow your painful experiences and weaknesses to turn you toward God; in other words, use your wounds and weaknesses for his glory.

2. PURSUE THE TRUTH

Second, be relentlessly committed to pursuing truth—both biblical truth and the truth regarding your own heart with its predilections and tendency to be manipulative and engage in self-deception. When we see ourselves through the grace-filled eyes of Jesus, it frees us to be honest with ourselves, God, and others. A fundamental hallmark of a Christian is that he or she loves the truth, wherever the truth leads. The ninth commandment tells us to not bear false witness against our neighbor. It follows that we ought not to bear false witness against ourselves as well. In counseling, I often encourage people to be honest with themselves about their thoughts and feelings. I gently remind them that we are called to "speak the truth in love," and that this applies to our own feelings of insecurity, anger, depression, anxiety, and other emotions we find unacceptable to admit and attempt to disown. Truth and honesty are essential and the starting point in the process of repentance.

3. REFLECT ON THE MOTIVES OF YOUR HEART

Third, commit yourself to be ruthlessly honest with yourself about yourself. The apostle Paul exhorts everyone "not to think of himself more highly than he ought to think, but to think with sober judgment, each according to the measure of faith that God has assigned" (Romans 12:3). A biblical response to our ruling passions requires thinking deeply about and having an accurate assessment of the heart motivations that drive us—even when that assessment is painful. Prayerful self-reflection is vital because we cannot repent of motives and behaviors of which we are unaware. It requires courage to admit, for example, that we avoid certain experiences such as rejection, embarrassment, and being alone, or that we love being the center of attention. King David deeply reflected on his abuse of power, adultery, and murder, but as Scott Sauls observed, he "did not shield himself from hard truths" (1 Samuel 12:13).[2] So, for example, when I observe that the motivations of my heart are manipulative, selfish, or unloving, I need to admit this with particularity and invite God into the process to both comfort me and give me the desire, courage, and ability to change. Be courageous as you reflect on what circumstances and experiences shaped you and caused you to make vows about the way you will live. We can trust that God is faithful and good and "will bring to light what is hidden in darkness and will expose the motives of the heart" (1 Corinthians 4:5 NIV).

A perfect prayer to begin this process is David's powerful prayer: "Search me, O God, and know my heart! Try me and know my thoughts! And see if there be any grievous way in me, and lead me in the way everlasting!" (Psalm 139:23–24). This prayer is particularly applicable because, as we have seen, our ruling passions can hurt others and sabotage our life, ministry, and relationships.

4. OBSERVE AND ASK ABOUT YOUR IMPACT

Fourth, *observe* how you interact with others, particularly those who are closest to you. What do you do with them? What is your impact on them? What do they feel when they are around you? How do you desire people to respond to you? How do you want to be perceived?

Those who are in the closest relationships with us will feel the negative impact of our ruling passions most acutely. If you want to know your ruling passions and are brave enough, ask for feedback.[3] If you're willing and humble, those closest to you may be in the best position to provide you with valuable insight into your ruling passions.

A simple example of how our ruling passions impact those closest to us came very early in my marriage. My wife, Miho, and I had been married for about a year when we flew to Boston for a vacation. Lobster is my favorite food, so I found a seafood restaurant and called ahead to reserve a five-pound lobster. As we drove to the restaurant, I anticipated a lovely dinner with my lovely wife. Actually, it's more honest to say, I anticipated a lovely dinner with my lovely lobster. I love lobster—I love food—too much. I grew up in a house of chaos with a physically intimidating older brother who often stole my food off my plate, so I can be very possessive about food. The thought of having my own five-pound lobster was bliss.

Honestly, as I now reflect on my motives as I began our conversation on the way to the restaurant, I realize I had no intention of sharing my lobster with anybody. Still, I asked Miho, "What are you going to order? You can have anything you want." Miho replied, "Dave, you're getting a five-pound lobster. I'll just have some of that." I may have twitched. I don't think I did, but I may have. I answered calmly and evenly, "You can get anything on the menu; don't worry about the price." I did not want to share my lobster. Miho is frugal, sensible, and practical. She seemed confused. "There is no way you can eat five pounds of lobster. I'll just have a few bites." I kept reiterating, "You can have anything on the menu, anything you want." She would retort, "That's ridiculous, why would we order another lobster?" We began to argue.

At the time, I had little self-awareness; I did not see my selfishness, my obsession with food, my desire for control, how manipulative I could be, or the impact on Miho as I presented myself as reasonable and made her out to be the crazy one. By the time we got to the parking lot, we were in a huge fight. We spent at least twenty minutes of our vacation arguing over whether I was going to give her a few bites of my lobster. At a certain point, she said, "I don't even want to eat with you; you're nuts. Drop me off at the hotel." Eventually, we made our way into the restaurant, where we sat icily staring at each other. Then our waitress approached.

"Excuse me, sir, did you order the big lobster?"

"Yes."

"Well, I have good news and bad news for you. The bad news is that when you reserved the five-pound lobster, I failed to check and see if we had one. I'm sorry to tell you that we don't have any five-pound lobsters."

Silence. "What's the good news?"

"The good news is that we have a ten-pound lobster, and if you want it, we will honor the same price we quoted you for the five-pound lobster." Needless to say, we didn't order a second lobster.

I share this story to illustrate the fact that my wife was feeling the negative, exasperating impact of one of my ruling passions. In the brief time we had been married, she had already experienced underlying issues that had permeated my life and leaked out onto her—a tendency to make sure my needs were satisfied or present myself as the good guy when I was the one being prideful and manipulative. Although my words sounded generous, she sensed how disingenuous I was. Miho cared for me by holding up a mirror to expose the selfish motivations of my heart and by not enabling *more* manipulative behavior. While it is painful to hear, receiving honest feedback is a huge gift because it gives us an opportunity to engage in meaningful repentance.

One of the most direct ways to get feedback about our impact on others is to *ask* those who are close to us. Ask your spouse, children, trusted friends, staff, and congregants to provide you with honest feedback. Here are some questions to consider asking:

- What effect do I have on you? How do I impact you?
- How do you feel when you are around me?
- Do you feel pressure to come through for me? If so, how? What do I do to create that pressure?

- Do you feel used or manipulated by me? If so, how?
- Do you feel pressure to be a certain way when you are around me?
- Am I arrogant? Dictatorial? Unreasonably demanding?
- Do you feel taken advantage of?
- Do you feel cared for? Loved? When?

If you are in ministry, consider asking staff members or congregants the following questions:

- What do I do well? What do I do poorly?
- What do you see as critical weaknesses in the way I lead, relate to others, preach, or engage in ministry?
- Do you see any issues in the way I treat my spouse, children, staff, or people over whom I have authority?
- Do you see any landmines in my life or ministry that could potentially sabotage me?

These questions are not for the faint of heart. It takes a lot of courage to ask them, and even more courage to *listen* without defending ourselves or explaining why we act in a certain way. We often miss these learning experiences by being prickly, defensive, or too proud to listen. Be prepared for some hard answers. We may not like what we hear. However, the gift of honest feedback will help us identify ruling passions that are hidden from our sight, provide insight into how they negatively affect those we love, and provide motivation to seek God for heart transformation.

5. RESIST YOUR RESISTANCE

Fifth, be on the lookout for your heart to resist transformation. Sometimes this resistance comes in the form of unbiblical responses to ruling passions, as described in our next chapter. Sometimes we experience resistance from internal factors such as our sinful nature and our ambivalence toward real transformation. In Psalm 119, the psalmist recognizes that we need God to incline us toward him and his will when he prays, "Incline my heart to your testimonies, and not to selfish gain!" (Psalm 119:36). The apostle Paul recognizes our tendency to resist doing the right thing and our need for God when he writes,

> For I have the desire to do what is right, but not the ability to carry it out. For I do not do the good I want, but the evil I do not want is what I keep on doing. . . . For I delight in the law of God, in my inner being, but I see in my members another law waging war against the law of my mind and making me captive to the law of sin that dwells in my members. (Romans 7:18–19, 22–23)

So, too, there is a part of me that does not want to change, be submitted to, and obey God fully. I need God to incline my heart toward him, even when I am conscious of resisting him. My prayer is "Help me to *want* to want you." Being aware of our tendency to resist change is essential as we embark on the transformation process. Chapter 12 addresses additional forms of resistance to change.

6. BE PREPARED FOR SPIRITUAL WARFARE

Finally, the reality of the Christian life is that we often deal with unseen forces—what Paul describes as "spiritual forces of evil" and "schemes of the devil" (Ephesians 6:11–12). As Paul Tripp has observed, spiritual warfare "is splashed across almost every page of Scripture, and because it is, it is a sobering warning to each one of us. Life, right here, right now, really is a moment-by moment spiritual war."[4] An essential aspect of preparing our hearts for transformation is developing discernment in how the Accuser may interact with us as we seek to rule our passions so that our one overarching passion is the supremacy of Christ.

One of the fundamental presuppositions of Scripture is the existence of good and evil, truth and lies. Jesus identifies Satan as the "father of lies," of whom Jesus says, "He was a murderer from the beginning, not holding to the truth, for there is no truth in him. When he lies, he speaks his native language, for he is a liar" (John 8:44 NIV). The main scheme of the devil is to make false assertions and to get you to believe those lies. People tell lies to each other and to themselves, but the genesis of those lies is the Evil One.

When Jesus asks his disciples, "Who do you say that I am?" Peter replies, "You are the Christ, the Son of the living God" (Matthew 16:15–16). Jesus praises Peter for this answer, saying, "Blessed are you, Simon Bar-Jonah! For flesh and blood has not revealed this to you, but my Father who is in heaven" (Matthew 16:17). In other words, Peter believed the truth, as revealed by God, and correspondingly answered with the truth.

Yet in the same chapter, Jesus then tells the disciples that he is about to suffer, be killed, and then raised from the dead (Matthew 16:21). In response to this truth, Peter rebukes Jesus and says, "Far be it from you, Lord! This shall never happen to you" (v. 22). In response, Jesus says to Peter, "Get behind me, Satan! You are a hindrance to me. For you are not setting your mind on the things of God, but on the things of man" (v. 23).

Isn't it interesting that Jesus, who had just noted that the truth behind Peter's identifying Jesus as the Son of God was from God, now addresses Peter as Satan? Why? It is obvious that Peter was not Satan, nor did he turn into Satan. Yet Jesus addressed Peter *as if* Satan was speaking through him. I believe that Jesus was addressing the energizing force behind Peter's false idea (which was that Jesus was *not* to suffer and be killed) because that lie violated God's will and was not true. The false idea verbalized by Peter originated from Satan. An idea is false when it contradicts the nature of God, God's will, or God's character. This passage teaches that the animating force behind a false idea is Satan. Decades later, perhaps remembering this incident, Peter warned us to be "sober-minded; be watchful. Your adversary the devil prowls around like a roaring lion, seeking someone to devour" (1 Peter 5:8).

As you prepare to identify and repent of your ruling passions, be mindful that Satan will feed you lies—twisting God's truth about your identity, skewing your ideas of what is most important in life, and leading you away from the bedrock reality of God's absolute and unconditional love for you. In contrast, Jesus identified himself as "the way, and the truth, and the life" (John 14:6). He further instructed his followers to abide in his word and promised, "If you abide in my word, you are truly my disciples, and you will *know the truth*, and the truth will set you free" (John 8:31–32).

As we will see in chapter 17, understanding, believing, and living according to the truth is an essential requirement to experiencing transformation. It takes time and wisdom to unravel the lies we believe about God, ourselves, relationships, our experiences, and the meaning that we ascribe to those experiences. Engaging in spiritual warfare is not merely praying or casting out demons; it involves deeply pondering and prudently applying the truth to our hearts.

How are we to regard spiritual warfare? We are not to attribute all things to Satan, nor are we to ignore him. Rather, as summed up by David Powlison, Satan plays an "underlying, behind-the-scenes role in the everyday problems of sin, misery, and death. . . . The way you pay attention to Satan is analogous to how you pay attention to other influencing factors: bodily problems, personal history, cultural and peer influences, situational stressors, and sufferings."[5] Be aware that the Evil One is the ultimate source of false beliefs, and prayerfully take a holistic approach to discerning what transformation looks like in your situation.[6]

REFLECTION QUESTIONS

1. As you reflect on the six ways to prepare your heart (Pray, Pursue the Truth, Reflect on the Motives of Your Heart, Observe and Ask About Your Impact, Resist Your Resistance, and Be Prepared for Spiritual Warfare), which of these come most naturally for you? Which are most challenging? Why?
2. Do you find honestly discerning and addressing the motives of your heart to be challenging? Why? What is difficult about this?
3. Identify a safe person in your life (trusted friend, adviser, counselor, spouse) of whom you can ask one or more of the following questions to help determine the impact you have on others.
   - What effect do I have on you? How do I impact you?
   - How do you feel when you are around me?
   - Do you feel pressure to come through for me? If so, how? What do I do to create that pressure?
   - Do you ever feel used or manipulated by me? If so, how?
   - Do you feel pressure to be a certain way when you are around me?
   - Am I arrogant? Dictatorial? Unreasonably demanding?
   - Do you feel taken advantage of?
   - Do you feel cared for? Loved? When?
4. If you are in pastoral ministry or are a ministry leader, go to a staff member or congregant of your ministry and ask the following questions:

- What do I do well? What do I do poorly?
- What do you see as critical weaknesses in the way I lead, relate to others, preach, or engage in ministry?
- Do you see any issues in the way I treat my spouse, children, staff, or people over whom I have authority?
- Do you see any landmines in my life or ministry that could potentially sabotage me or my ministry?

5. If you find yourself resisting the above exercises, what is the reason for your resistance? What specific steps can/will you take to overcome your resistance?

Chapter 12
ADDRESSING OUR RESISTANCES

We are often interested in transformation, but sometimes ironically find ourselves resisting the very change we long for or the ways God uses to change us. Resistance to change comes in many forms. Let's examine five common forms of resistance and objections I have encountered. These are negative ways we tend to respond to our weaknesses, our predilections, and our ruling passions. As you read through these responses, examine whether you have engaged in these as you have been reading this book.

1. DENYING WHAT REALLY RULES US

Denial is a powerful thing. We tend to deny our sinful ruling passions, much in the way that an alcoholic denies his addiction. Or we avoid self-awareness and deceive ourselves by telling ourselves that we don't really have any ruling passions. It's easier to deny our issues than to go "below the waterline," where we must explore and feel our pain, fears, crushed longings, and disappointments and examine the motives of our hearts. Admittedly, it's not easy or comfortable to do the deep, below-the-surface work of looking at ourselves honestly. It can be quite disorienting and painful to become aware of our own less-than-pure motives and realize that our motives are not as noble as we have believed. Many of us would rather live in blissful denial where it feels much safer than developing self-awareness that can shatter our glittering self-image.

2. DESPISING OUR RULING PASSIONS AND ENGAGING IN SELF-LOATHING

Sometimes when we are brave enough to admit our ruling passions, we despise ourselves for having them; this can lead to self-loathing. This is particularly true if we feel weak or vulnerable. For example, when John, the ministry leader in chapter 7 who had been punished by his father and forced to sit outside in girls' clothes, recognized his longing for love and admiration, he felt shame for feeling weak and needy. His longing to be admired brought on feelings of deep humiliation rather than compassion for himself and his own needs. It was sad to observe him wrestle with his emotions. One moment, he would have tears in his eyes as he expressed his longing for affirmation that he never received from his cruel father. Then, the next moment he would shift and become angry at himself for being weak and needy. With complete self-disdain he would say, "I'm just a slug." He despised his longing, rather than recognizing it as a real, normal, and universal human need. The problem is that engaging in self-loathing and despising our longings is not healthy or productive. It tends to create a cycle of self-sabotage and self-destruction rather than generating real heart change. It also ignores the grace of God and his unconditional love for us.

3. INDULGING OUR RULING PASSIONS

A third unhealthy approach to addressing our ruling passions is to indulge them. We might rationalize why we have our particular ruling passions with statements such as "That's just the way I am," "I just have a bad temper," or "I'm naturally shy." However, our natural disposition is never a justification for failing to repent of sinful attitudes or conduct. When we indulge our ruling passions, we are using them as an excuse to stay stuck in sinful patterns of behavior. Such an attitude ignores our sinful human inclinations from which we ought to repent. It also ignores God's plan of sanctification for us—to be changed into the image of Christ.

4. PSEUDO-SPIRITUALIZING OUR RULING PASSIONS

Another common and insidious response is to "spiritualize" our ruling passions with facile, pseudo-scriptural rationalizations. This takes different forms. You may have heard statements like these:

- "I don't need to look deeply at my past or my motives or the sinfulness of my heart. The Bible tells me that I'm not to look to the past, because, like Paul in Philippians 3:13–14, 'forgetting what lies behind and straining forward to what lies ahead, I press on toward the goal for the prize of the upward call of God in Christ Jesus.'"
- "That's the old man—I'm a 'new creation' in Christ Jesus."
- "By faith I don't have any ruling passions contrary to God's rule in my life."
- "We don't need to engage in 'psychobabble.' Just read your Bible."

Responses like these can arise from a misunderstanding of Scripture or can be forms of denial to help avoid seeing the sinful nature of our own hearts and motives or avoid the pain of honestly processing emotional wounds. Often, we can be guilty of using Scripture the way a magician might make an incantation—speaking magical words that we believe will automatically and instantaneously change ourselves or our circumstances. Speak it into existence, and *poof*—you are changed! Oh, that it were that easy!

Unfortunately, engaging in these types of pseudo-spiritual practices and responses is as dangerous as putting a Band-Aid over a cancerous tumor. We do so at our own peril because it puts us at increased risk of allowing the ruling passion to metastasize while allowing us to have the appearance of being biblical and spiritual in the process. The process of sanctification is a deep work of God in our hearts that takes time, honesty, a commitment to change, deep reflection, patience, and prayer. It does involve suffering, but it is a suffering that leads to maturity (James 1:2–5).

5. PROTECTING OUR RULING PASSIONS

The most insidious response to our ruling passions is to protect them. Some guard their ruling passions as if they were untouchable treasures rather than cancer to be rooted out. If anyone comments on them or gets too close, they take offense—and cut them off. "Don't go there." Considering this, many are content to leave them untouched by the power of Christ when, in fact, it is the power of Christ that heals and sets us free.

We need to be aware of these five unbiblical responses and avoid them. They are traps and will lead us into greater blindness regarding our deceitful hearts. Ultimately, they will lead us to harden our hearts against the truth. Instead, we are in desperate need of heart and mind transformation. We need to be radically willing to honestly examine our hearts and reorder our passions so that Christ is Lord of our hearts and his priorities become our priorities so that we willingly walk in obedience to him.

REFLECTION QUESTIONS

1. Which of the unbiblical responses discussed in this chapter are most applicable to you? Do you tend to deny, despise, indulge, spiritualize, or protect your ruling passions?
2. What are specific ways you indulge your ruling passions? What is your motive for doing so? How has this impacted others in your life?
3. How do these unbiblical responses keep you from addressing your ruling passions? How does that impact your spiritual growth?
4. How do these unbiblical responses keep others from knowing you or knowing your heart? How does that impact your spiritual growth?
5. Imagine you were counseling a congregant or friend, and she says, "The Bible tells me that I'm not to look to the past because Paul said in Philippians 3:13–14, 'forgetting what lies behind and straining forward to what lies ahead, I press on toward the goal for the prize of the upward call of God in Christ Jesus.'" How would you respond to her?

Chapter 13
IDENTIFY OUR RULING PASSIONS AND LET CONFESSION BE OUR RESET

This and the following several chapters will guide us through a comprehensive examination of our lives by taking steps to understand and respond to our ruling passions. We will prayerfully explore the genesis of our ruling passions, including key experiences that have formed who we are today, and ask God to redeem our past experiences—even the painful wounds we have received and sinful choices we have made. We will be encouraged to turn to and trust Christ with our entire beings and walk in the truth of God's Word and the supremacy of Christ as our guide. In chapter 18 we will have the opportunity to further integrate these details into a personal narrative to see how our ruling passions operate in the context of our entire lives. In chapter 19 I share my story and how my ruling passions have shaped my life. I pray that as you interact and engage with each of these steps you will be inspired to ask God to effectuate deep transformation in your life.

By way of overview, here are the steps we will cover:

1. Identify and Confess Our Ruling Passions (chapter 13)
2. Ask God to Redeem Our Ruling Passions (chapter 14)
3. Process Emotions in a Godly and Healthy Way (chapter 15)
4. Let Christ Be Our Strength (chapter 16)
5. Walk in the Truth (chapter 17)

CONFESS YOUR RULING PASSIONS

The first step in biblically responding to ruling passions is to identify them and to develop a deep understanding of how they originated and have impacted our lives. We started the process of identifying our ruling passions in chapter 5. If you have not yet done so, please complete the Personal Worksheet on page 53 to help identify your ruling passions.

Having identified the vows we've made, we will explore the impact of our ruling passions and compose a prayer to acknowledge how they have impacted us and others and, where appropriate, confess them to the Lord. Our ruling passions can influence us both negatively and positively and can have a healthy and unhealthy impact on ourselves and others. They will influence how we organize our lives and determine whether we relate to others with a heart motivated out of love and service or out of self-serving manipulation. Here are some steps to take as we prepare to write our confession. Because our ruling passions are so personal to our lives, it is helpful to come up with specific examples of how they have played out in our lives. Although the examples below may seem minor, remember that ruling passions can permeate our lives in minor and major ways.

First, consider and acknowledge how your ruling passions have affected your life and the major decisions you have made. For example, a ruling passion to never fail may have had an impact on what schools you attended, your choice of occupations, whether to seek a promotion at work, and whether to engage in sports and recreational and social activities. A person who vows never to fail may stop himself from learning to dance, asking a person out for a date, or running for public office. With this ruling passion, Victoria avoided seeking a promotion for which she was highly qualified. Although she loved running, she refused to sign up for a marathon with her best friend because she feared performing poorly.

Second, consider how your vows may have affected your relationships with others. A vow to be the best in whatever one does may hurt those around us because we can become highly competitive, even where being the best does not matter or intimidates others in an unhelpful way. For example, when Bob taught his teenage children to play pickleball, he was unable to allow them to practice enough to develop their skills. Rather than helping them build their confidence by experiencing success or winning some games, his ruling passion to be the best caused him to dominate even practice sessions. And when he perceived himself as an inferior player, he became moody, silently sulked in a corner, or just walked out, leaving his children baffled and frustrated. Consumed with being the best, his impact on others was negative and damaging.

Third, consider how your ruling passion has affected your relationship with God. A ruling passion for avoiding loneliness can inspire one to seek a deeper relationship with God or cause one to seek relief through illicit conduct. Jeremy sought relief from loneliness by engaging in sexual relationships with women.

As you reflect on this step of confession, open your heart before the Lord and ask him to help you see clearly. We have nothing to fear and everything to gain as we come before our gracious, loving, and forgiving God. One of the most powerful promises in Scripture says, "If we confess our sins, he is faithful and just to forgive us our sins and to cleanse us from all unrighteousness" (1 John 1:9). I encourage you to fully write out your confession in a way that accounts for how your ruling passions have permeated many aspects of your life and affected others.

Here is an example of a detailed confession where the ruling passion is receiving affirmation:

> Lord, I confess that the ruling passion of my heart has been to seek affirmation. I acknowledge that this has had both a positive and negative impact on me and others. I have been sensitive to others and affirmed them because I know how hard it feels not to be affirmed. However, I also acknowledge that I have been disingenuous in affirming others because I have affirmed them when they underperformed; my motive was to look good in their eyes.
>
> I confess that seeking my own affirmation has become more of a priority in my life than you are. I have made seeking affirmation an ultimate commitment in my life. At certain times I seek affirmation from others more than I seek to follow and obey you. I confess that I have organized my world in both overt and subtle ways to get people to function for me so they are more likely to affirm me. This has led me to manipulate others to get them to affirm me, and by doing so, I have failed to love them well. I confess that by manipulating others, I have essentially used them, and this has hurt them. In some cases, it has damaged my relationships.
>
> I also confess that there have been times when I have compromised the truth because I longed for affirmation more than the truth. In so doing, I have let affirmation from others become more important than affirmation from you, Lord. I thank you for giving me the insight to

see this in my own heart. I pray that you will give me the ability to repent as I become more aware of this tendency. I ask for your forgiveness and for the power to change. Amen.

The following is a sample confession related to the pursuit of physical and emotional comfort as a ruling passion:

Lord, I confess that my ruling passion has been to seek and obtain physical and emotional comfort. I acknowledge that this has impacted my life in many ways. I have avoided situations that made me uncomfortable. When I was young, I did not go to overnight camp because I imagined being uncomfortable sleeping in bunk beds and did not attend social events when I believed it would make me feel awkward or insecure. I missed many opportunities that would have helped me to develop and become an emotionally mature, well-rounded person.

My ruling passion has also impacted others close to me; in many instances, I choose to serve myself rather than love and serve others. When my children wanted to go to the beach, or later when they desired to go on short-term mission trips to locations where I knew I would be out of my comfort zone, I came up with excuses to justify saying no to them. I now can see that I was dishonest with the excuses I gave and I deprived them of opportunities that would have helped them grow.

I acknowledge that I am squeamish when I'm in hospital settings where people are sick, and that being with people who are in pain or sick makes me feel so uncomfortable because I don't know how to respond to them. I confess that when my brother was terminally ill and had requested me to stay in the hospital room overnight with him, I allowed my ultimate commitment to my own comfort to control my response. My brother knew he was dying but because I prioritized my comfort, I failed to comfort him when he needed me during those final moments of his life.

As I reflect on dozens of instances in my life, I can see that obtaining comfort has been an ultimate commitment in my life and that I have organized my world and manipulated others to put myself first. I thank you for revealing this truth to me, for giving me clarity to see it, the courage to admit it, and the desire to change. I thank you that I can confess my sins to you and that you are gracious and forgive me. Amen.

The beautiful promise of the gospel is that God forgives us. He looks at us through the eyes of love and grace so that we need not shrink back and be ashamed. Scripture assures us that we are invited to enter God's presence to confess our sins with full confidence in his understanding, love, and grace. A beautiful passage from the book of Hebrews assures us of this:

> Since then we have a great high priest who has passed through the heavens, Jesus, the Son of God, let us hold fast our confession. For we do not have a high priest who is unable to sympathize with our weaknesses, but one who in every respect has been tempted as we are, yet without sin. Let us then with confidence draw near to the throne of grace, that we may receive mercy and find grace to help in time of need. (Hebrews 4:14–16)

REFLECTION QUESTIONS TO CONFESS YOUR RULING PASSIONS

1. Write out the vows that you have made (from chapter 5).
2. How have your ruling passions affected the significant decisions you've made in the way you live your life (e.g., educational, vocational, relational, marriage, parenting, ministry)? Be sure to reflect on past and present decisions.
3. How have your ruling passions affected your relationships with those who are closest to you? Consider your relationships with your spouse, children, close friends, church, and vocational community (e.g., "My ruling passion to be the expert has discouraged my son from engaging in deep conversations with me," or "My ruling passion to be a success in ministry has caused me to be jealous of subordinates and I have failed to affirm or promote them").
4. How have your ruling passions had an impact on your relationship with God? What opportunities have you said "no" or "yes" to that were driven by your ruling passions?
5. Prayerfully write out a detailed confession to God.

Chapter 14
ASK GOD TO REDEEM OUR PASSIONS

As we have seen in chapter 12, a common but unhealthy and destructive tendency is to deny, despise, indulge, spiritualize, or protect our ruling passions. A much more productive and godly response is to take God at his word and trust that he is the God of redemption who can transform our painful experiences, wounded hearts, and broken lives and use them for good in the future (Romans 8:28). It may be hard to imagine how God can redeem some of our most painful and difficult experiences. However, the Scriptures provide rich instances where God has brought beauty out of ashes. We will see that the apostle Paul is the quintessential example of a man who stewarded his past for the glory of God and lived out the truth of Romans 8:28.

BE A GODLY STEWARD OF YOUR PAST

As you've reflected on the genesis of your ruling passions, you have begun to understand that they are based on your life's experiences, choices you made, your longings, and your goals to protect yourself from pain or to attain safety, comfort, or pleasure. Ruling passions often develop from deep pain, relational wounds, our sinful behaviors, and being sinned against. Indeed, as Dan Allender puts it,

> Tragedy shapes our deepest passions, and our passions shape who we are and what we will become. Each person living in a fallen world will encounter abandonment, betrayal, and shame. . . . It's the necessary context in which we come to grips with how we will live. It is in the midst of affliction that we become our truest or most false self.[1]

How do we allow God to help us steward our most painful traumatic wounds and false beliefs and to help us walk in the truth so that our ruling passions are transformed and we are enabled to love God and others? We must ask God to heal our wounds and see the past experiences that have shaped us through a different lens—a lens that is thoroughly biblical and reflects God's redemptive purposes. This is not an easy journey. As Allender also shares,

> Reentering terrain we have fenced off as forbidden is an act of profound courage. It requires learning to read our story with the eyes that see as God sees. We grow in faith to the degree we do what seems counterintuitive: open our hearts to remember . . . and ask God to engage our heartache with tenderness.[2]

We simply can't ignore our wounds; we must remember and attend to them, appropriately grieve, and undergo a significant healing process.[3] Here is a profound, life-changing truth: You can't change your past, but *you can be a godly steward of your past and use your wounds as an opportunity for ministry.*[4]

Others have similarly noted that you can't change the beginning, but you have the responsibility to get a good ending. In other words, the past is always open to reinterpretation and can be formed and reformed in light of biblical truth and the redemptive character of God.

This is great news of hope for transformation: we do not have to be defined by our past. If we regard ourselves as being calcified in the process of spiritual formation, then we will be stuck in a story that is unresolved. But if we see ourselves undergoing dynamic change and being formed and transformed into mature, spiritually healthy leaders, there is great hope for the future. To go forward, we must go back to address formative experiences that are the seedbed for our ruling passions and wisely steward our past. As beloved priest and professor Henri Nouwen advises, "This is why, in all helping professions . . . the first questions are always directed to the memory of the . . . client." He advocates for asking the hurting person to tell their story and the events which led them to this place here and now. He continues, "It is clear that what . . . therapists hear about are not just events, but memories of events. It is no exaggeration to say that the suffering we most frequently encounter in the ministry is a suffering of memories."[5]

Many recoil at the idea of revisiting our painful past. *Why can't I just forget the past and move on? Why should I try to remember past events that hurt me or were humiliating? Won't doing so plunge me into the same pain, self-pity, or despair from which I am trying to escape?* As Richard Plass and James Cofield share, remembering our stories can be extremely difficult. Our stories are often filled with "sadness, anger, disgust, anxiety, guilt, fear, and shame. To revisit them is very painful."[6] And yet, as Rabbi Heschel states, "Much of what the Bible demands can be comprised in one imperative: Remember."[7] Henri

Nouwen's perspective on this is instructive and we would be wise to heed it:

> Forgetting the past is like turning our most intimate teacher against us. By refusing to face our painful memories we miss the opportunity to change our hearts and grow mature in repentance. When Jesus says, "It is not the healthy who need the doctor, but the sick" (Mark 2:17), He affirms that only those who face their wounded condition can be available for healing and so enter into a new way of living. . . . How are we healed of our wounding memories? We are healed first of all by letting them be available, by leading them out of the corner of forgetfulness and remembering them as part of our life stories. What is forgotten is unavailable, and what is unavailable cannot be healed.[8]

The idea of using your wounds as an opportunity for ministry comes straight out of Scripture. The apostle Paul is a model of a person who allowed God to redeem his past sinful behavior and traumatic experiences and then used his past as a springboard for loving God and ministering to others.

THE APOSTLE PAUL'S STEWARDSHIP OF TRAUMA

Consider how many traumatic events were suffered by the apostle Paul and how he handled his past painful experiences. Paul was

- *dragged* out of the city and *stoned* in Lystra (Acts 14);
- *abandoned* by ministry partners Barnabas and John Mark while embarking on a missionary journey (Acts 15);

- *harassed* by a girl with a spirit of divination for "many days" in Philippi (Acts 16);
- *beaten and jailed* in Philippi (Acts 16);
- in an *earthquake* while in jail (Acts 16);
- caught up in a *riot* in Thessalonica while his friend, Jason, was beaten and robbed (Acts 17);
- *ridiculed and mocked* by Athenian philosophers who sought to embarrass him (Acts 17);
- *arrested* in Corinth and *dragged* before the court (Acts 18);
- in a *riot* in Ephesus where his friends were seized, beaten, and persecuted (Acts 19);
- the subject of a *plot to kill* him (Acts 20);
- *arrested* at the Temple in Jerusalem (Acts 21);
- *beaten* by crowds who attempt to kill him in Jerusalem (Acts 21);
- the recipient of *death threats* and another *plot to kill* him (Acts 23);
- *jailed* in Caesarea (Felix) (Acts 23);
- *kept languishing* in jail in Caesarea (Acts 24);
- *ridiculed* by Agrippa while giving testimony (Acts 26);
- nearly lost in a *storm and shipwrecked* in the Mediterranean (Acts 27);
- almost *murdered* when the soldiers decided to *kill all prisoners*, including Paul (Acts 27);
- *bitten by a deadly snake* in Malta (Acts 28);
- *imprisoned* in Rome (Acts 28); and
- *sentenced to death* (Acts 28; Philippians 1; see also 2 Corinthians 11:23–28).

Unless we have endured some form of trauma, it's easy to underestimate the power of the images that must have been seared into Paul's memory, and the paralyzing terror and helplessness he must have experienced. We have been desensitized to the impact of trauma in our age of visual media because we have been exposed to thousands of movie scenes filled with violence, destruction, war, and death. In short, like many today, Paul was the recipient of physical and emotional abuse.

Additionally, Paul was not only the *recipient* of painful traumas, but he was also an agent of evil before his conversion; he intentionally sinned against God and persecuted believers, even approving of their imprisonment and death (Acts 8:1; 9:1–5). Although Paul describes himself as having been "a blasphemer, persecutor, and insolent opponent" of Christians, he experienced radical transformation because "the grace of our Lord overflowed for me with the faith and love that are in Christ Jesus" (1 Timothy 1:12–14).

What can we learn from Paul? He had to attend to his painful memories and the guilt that accompanied them. On the one hand, he had to hold the painful memory that he had persecuted Christ and Christians, and on the other hand, he allowed his thinking to be transformed and his memories to be redeemed for God's glory. Rather than stuffing his memories or letting his past sins, wounds, and traumas define or paralyze him, he allowed them to be the basis *from which he ministered comfort to others* (2 Corinthians 1:4). Paul was a godly steward of his painful experiences and used them as opportunities for ministry.

So where do we start in redeeming our memories? How can memories that have caused us the very pain that we want to avoid be used for good? What does it mean to steward our memories in a way that honors God and our past?

HEALTHY AND UNHEALTHY MEMORIES

We need to first recognize the difference between healthy and unhealthy memories. Here are two definitions that I have found extremely helpful as we ask God to redeem our past wounds, sins, and traumatic events. A "healthy memory" is a recollection of a past event that increases my commitment to love God and others. In contrast, an "unhealthy memory" is a recollection of a past event that is used to justify disobeying God or used to serve me in the present.[9] Any one of the many traumatic incidents Paul endured could have created a state of fear and anxiety that could have stopped him from accomplishing his mission. Any one of them could have resulted in a memory that he could have used to justify disobeying God and serving himself, rather than those he was called to evangelize and the churches he was called to plant. Any experience could have been used to create a ruling passion of seeking security and safety had he not allowed God to redeem his past and engage in a healthy healing process. But Paul maintained healthy memories of his past. How did Paul do this? Paul engaged in three important practices to maintain healthy memories of these traumatic events: reflect, communicate, and reexpose.[10]

First, Paul was willing to *relive the painful events by intentionally reflecting* on his past traumatic experiences. Consider how difficult and painful it is to remember past conversations, events, and incidents that cause pain. Paul did not deny or dismiss these traumas; he intentionally reflected on them. This enabled him to discern, in part, how his painful experiences were part of God's redemptive and purposeful plan. And he comes to one conclusion: to not rely on himself, "but on God":

> We do not want you to be uninformed, brothers and sisters, about the troubles we experienced in the province of Asia. We were under great pressure, far beyond our ability

to endure, so that we despaired of life itself. Indeed, we felt we had received the sentence of death. But this happened that we might not rely on ourselves but on God, who raises the dead. (2 Corinthians 1:8–9 NIV)

Second, Paul was willing to communicate with others about his past experiences to strengthen their faith. In his letter to the Corinthian church, he recounts the trauma he has endured in the past:

> Five times I received at the hands of the Jews the forty lashes less one. Three times I was beaten with rods. Once I was stoned. Three times I was shipwrecked; a night and a day I was adrift at sea; on frequent journeys, in danger from rivers, danger from robbers, danger from my own people, danger from Gentiles, danger in the city, danger in the wilderness, danger at sea, danger from false brothers; in toil and hardship, through many a sleepless night, in hunger and thirst, often without food, in cold and exposure. And, apart from other things, there is the daily pressure on me of my anxiety for all the churches. (2 Corinthians 11:24–28)

Paul does not feel sorry for himself or harbor bitterness toward those who traumatized him. Rather, his motivation is to help those to whom he is writing, knowing that they, too, will endure hardships. All of us have stories to tell of our own struggles that can benefit and bless those with whom we share them.

Paul's recounting is shame-free. Paul is willing to engage in self-disclosure of his personal struggles and sinful behavior. He recounts the anxieties he experienced over his concern for the churches (2 Corinthians 11:28), and that he "persecuted the church of God violently and tried to destroy it" (Galatians 1:13).

Sometimes our past includes events or behaviors that feel shameful, but when shared with others, they can be a loving, sacrificial and immeasurable gift to others, serving to encourage, edify, and build their faith. How many people are helped when those who have struggled with abuse, addictions, and sinful behavior have disclosed their sins, both their victories and failures? King David committed rape, adultery, and murder. David disclosed his sin and wrote about it in the Psalms (e.g., Psalm 51). God has used David's self-disclosure for the benefit of countless readers over thousands of years.

Years before we were married, a serial killer raped my wife, Miho. She kept this hidden from me for the first fifteen years of our marriage. However, after resolving to allow God to redeem her past and to use this trauma for God's glory, she created a one-woman performance entitled *Clean Sheets*, in which she reveals the rape and how God used that in her life to bring her to faith. Miho has performed *Clean Sheets* around the world for thousands of people, bringing to light that which was previously hidden and shameful. Her willingness to disclose her deeply painful, traumatic personal experiences has helped many to have renewed faith and hope. Being a good steward of our past means sharing our struggles with others to give them courage and hope.

Finally, Paul *reexposes himself* to the same kinds of situations, people, and events that traumatized him in the past to love them and serve God.[11] Paul was stoned and dragged out of the city by the mob, and yet he got up and *went back into the same city*, the place of trauma (Acts 14:19–20). Then Paul and Barnabas returned to other cities where he had been traumatized: "strengthening the souls of the disciples, encouraging them to continue in the faith" (Acts 14:21–22; see also 1 Thessalonians 2:2).

Remarkably, although he was ridiculed and mocked by unbelievers, Paul returned to debate them (Acts 17); although he was arrested and jailed, he exposed himself to be arrested again (Acts 18; 21); although he was severely beaten, he returned to the same circumstances and risked repeated beatings (Acts 16; 21); and although he was shipwrecked, he returned to the sea (2 Corinthians 11:25; Acts 27). What enabled Paul to reexpose himself to the same danger and people who tried to harm him? Paul understood the power and purpose of his past and stewarded his pain and afflictions to comfort others (2 Corinthians 1:3–8).

This is the acid test of allowing God to redeem our past. Are we willing to use our memories of painful events and—when it is wise and appropriate—reexpose ourselves to the same situations where we were hurt so that our experiences might prove redemptive to those around us?[12] After Moses fled from Egypt after committing murder, he left the safety of his home in Midian and returned to identify with his fellow Jews (Exodus 2:11–22; 4:20). Joseph resumed his relationship with his brothers even though they had dealt so treacherously with him. And Paul returned to share the gospel with his persecutors. Are we willing to forgive those who have hurt us in the same way that Christ forgave those who persecuted and killed him? No doubt some of the same people in Jerusalem who mocked Jesus as he was forced to carry his cross to Golgotha and were present at his crucifixion were also present when Peter preached the gospel in Acts 2. As Peter was preaching this sermon, he may have been looking into the eyes of those who spit on Jesus or demanded his crucifixion. Still, Peter was willing to preach the good news of Christ to those who offended him deeply (Acts 2:36–39).

We are called to do no less. To allow God to redeem our past painful experiences, including our sinful acts, we must be willing to ask God to see our past through a biblically compassionate, grace-filled, and redemptive lens, and for a fresh vision of how to be a godly steward of our past. How can we do this? In the next chapter, we will examine the practical steps we can take to redeem our painful experiences, wounded hearts, and broken lives.

REFLECTION QUESTIONS

1. Do you agree with Henri Nouwen's perspective that "Forgetting the past is like turning our most intimate teacher against us. By refusing to face our painful memories, we miss the opportunity to change our hearts and grow mature in repentance"? Why or why not?
2. How have you approached your painful memories? Do you tend to stuff them and try to forget them? Are you willing to relive and disclose them for a redemptive purpose?
3. An "unhealthy memory" is a recollection of a past event that is used to justify disobeying God or to serve ourselves in the present. Are there ways you have used memories in an unhealthy way to justify serving yourself or sinning against God? Give some examples.
4. A "healthy memory" is a recollection of a past event that increases our commitment to love God and others. Are there ways you have used memories in a healthy way to love God and others? Give some examples.
5. Paul experienced multiple traumas, tragedies, and disappointments during his years of ministry and yet was a good steward of his past. What kind of events in your life have you experienced that you could steward well for God's glory and in service to others?

Chapter 15
PROCESS EMOTIONS IN A GODLY AND HEALTHY WAY

An essential part of the healing and redemptive process is to address our emotions in a godly, healthy way. The range of suffering in our lives can be enormous. Far too many in our churches have had difficult, even horrendous, experiences where abuse, tragedies, trauma, losses, and cruelty have resulted in deep wounds. Most of us have not been equipped to tend to our wounded hearts well. There are at least three reasons for this.

First, our family of origin is the primary place where we learn about our emotions. Each family has spoken or unspoken rules about emotions and whether emotions are considered dangerous and untrustworthy or normal and good. We learn whether it is safe and appropriate to feel and express our emotions or whether we must deny, suppress, and hide them. Most have heard a parent say, "Stop crying, or I'll give you something to cry about" or "If you can't say something nice, don't say anything at all." Many have grown up in environments where it simply was not safe to feel or express one's feelings. Whatever we have learned in our families of origin, we bring into the church. Ministry leaders do the same, and we must model and teach a healthy biblical approach to our emotions.[1]

Second, many don't have a biblical theology of emotions. A sad casualty is that many Christians have been taught to deny or pay little attention to their emotions because feelings are often seen as untrustworthy or even sinful. Great emphasis is placed on what we "know" to be true, or we are encouraged to "walk by faith, not by feelings." This view leaves no room for emotions, particularly anxiety, sadness, or anger. Some have been taught that we are not supposed to experience sadness because, for example, Paul commands us to "rejoice in the Lord," or that we are not supposed to feel anxiety because Paul commands us to "not be anxious about anything" (Philippians 4:4, 6). Thinking that we can simply ignore or avoid our emotions, we stuff or deny them and then claim that we have peace. Peter Scazzero points out, by inflating "ourselves with a false confidence to make [the disowned] feelings go away. . . . We quote Scripture, pray Scripture, memorize Scripture—anything to keep ourselves from being overwhelmed by those feelings."[2]

As a result of our poor theology, we often cope by burying painful memories and trying to move on without addressing our wounds. This is not biblical. As noted by Dan Allender and Tremper Longman,

> Ignoring our emotions is turning our back on reality. Listening to our emotions ushers us into reality. And reality is where we meet God . . . Emotions are the language of the soul. They are the cry that gives the heart a voice. . . . In neglecting our intense emotions, we are false to ourselves and lose a wonderful opportunity to know God. We forget that change comes through brutal honesty and vulnerability before God.[3]

Neglecting or denying our emotions is a recipe for further pain. Emotions that are buried will resurface and manifest themselves in other, more detrimental ways. Scazzero states, "To the degree that we are unable to express our emotions, we remain impaired in our ability to love God, others, and ourselves well. . . . To cut them out of our spirituality is to slice off an essential part of our humanity."[4]

Third, many Christians and ministry leaders engage in a process known as "spiritual bypass," which is using God, Scripture, spiritual ideas, and practices to *avoid* facing emotional pain, unresolved emotional or relational issues, trauma, psychological wounds, and difficult, complex issues.[5] Spiritual bypass occurs when, for example, instead of grieving the death of a loved one, we leap over the painful feelings of loss and the grieving process to the intellectual conclusion that our loved one is in heaven, or immediately quote a Scripture such as Romans 8:28. Or we explain away difficult emotions of sadness, anger, and anxiety as either spiritual attacks of the enemy or as a "work of the flesh," rather than squarely facing the emotional turmoil or disturbing situation we may be facing. Although it is true that our loved one is in heaven and all things "do work together for good," spiritual bypass literally "bypasses" the necessary steps of allowing ourselves to feel the painful emotions or address the complex issues that we are facing. What makes spiritual bypass more insidious is that when we engage in it, we can sound spiritual, scriptural, and mature. People also can applaud us for our "strong faith."

Spiritual bypass can mask emotional immaturity; engaging in this practice can lead to severe consequences for our well-being. We learn to cut off our emotions rather than feeling them; we learn not to live in the reality of the present; we bear false witness to the truth of what is really happening inside us; we become unable to empathetically feel the emotional pain of others; and we often will develop physical symptoms from our suppressed emotions in form of ulcers, back pain, and panic attacks, to name a few.

As ministry leaders, the consequences of engaging in spiritual bypass to our families and congregants are spiritually damaging. We present a facade of spiritual maturity and model false narratives about how others should experience and process their grief, and then others emulate this harmful practice. Engaging in spiritual bypass can be deadly to physical and spiritual health. A person who has a terminal disease and claims that "by faith, I'm not sick" may fail to get life-saving treatment. When we teach those we lead to engage in spiritual bypass, they are deprived of knowing their hearts and experiencing true intimacy with Christ. Ultimately, when people experience the impact of spiritual bypass in their own lives or the lives of their leaders, it can be so discouraging that it leads to deconstructing their faith or giving it up altogether, concluding that "Christianity does not work."

To escape the consequences of these three approaches to pain, we need a wise, accurate biblical theology of emotion.

GOD CAN'T HEAL WHAT YOU WON'T FEEL

Scripture describes God as an emotional being who feels a wide variety of emotions.[6] God is described as loving (Deuteronomy 7:7–8; Jeremiah 31:3), joyful (Jeremiah 32:41; Zephaniah 3:17), jealous (Exodus 20:5), angry (Ezekiel 5:13), regretful (Genesis 6:6), pleased (1 Kings 3:10), compassionate (Psalm 103:13), and sorrowful (Matthew 26:37–38). As image bearers, we, too, are made as complex beings with the capacity to deeply feel a myriad of emotions.[7] The Bible contains intensely emotional language and is filled with examples of people being honest about their emotions, ranging from worshipful joy to the depths of despair and darkness. Denying that we have emotions does great harm to ourselves and misrepresents the teaching of Scripture. The ability to feel emotions is a "gift from God . . . [a] source of intelligence, faith, and love."[8]

For example, one major lesson from the Psalms is how to express our deepest emotions honestly to God. The Psalms are filled with a broad expression of emotions. In Psalm 6, David does not cover his emotions; he honestly expresses his pain and sadness directly to God. Notice the graphic language David uses in his prayer:

> Be gracious to me, O LORD, for I am *languishing*; heal me, O LORD, for my bones are *troubled*. My soul also is *greatly troubled*. But you, O LORD—how long? Turn, O LORD, deliver my life; save me for the sake of your steadfast love. . . . I am *weary with my moaning*; every night I flood my bed with *tears*; I drench my couch with my *weeping*. My eye *wastes away* because of *grief*; it grows weak because of all my foes. (Psalm 6:2–7)

In Psalm 88 we observe the writer's honesty, not only about his pain but also his perceptions that God may have caused his agony:

> O LORD, God of my salvation, I cry out day and night before you. Let my prayer come before you; incline your ear to my cry! For my soul is full of troubles . . . *You have put me* in the depths of the pit, in the regions dark and deep. *Your wrath* lies heavy upon me, and *you overwhelm* me with all your waves. *You have caused* my companions to shun me; *you have made me* a horror to them. . . . Every day I call upon you, O LORD; I spread out my hands to you. . . . O LORD, why do *you cast my soul away*? Why *do*

you hide your face from me? . . . I suffer *your terrors*; I am helpless. Your wrath has swept over me; *your dreadful assaults* destroy me. (Psalm 88:1-3, 6-9, 14-16)

Many would be uncomfortable expressing such thoughts in prayer, or even hearing them prayed. If you were counseling this psalmist, would you advise him not to express his emotions to God in this way? Would you tell him not to feel so badly, encourage him to walk by faith and not feelings, or admonish him for having deficient theology? Would you insist that "God is good, even when you feel so terrible"? The psalmists' honest prayers are recorded in Scripture to help us understand that we can and should feel our emotions and honestly express them to God.

After receiving the terrible news that his children had been killed and that he had lost his wealth, Job "got up and tore his robe" and "fell to the ground." Yet, Scripture also tells us that "in all this, Job did not sin" (Job 1:20, 22 NIV). In his work on suffering, Tim Keller notes that "Job's grief was expressed with powerful emotion and soaring rhetoric. Job did not 'make nice' with God, praying politely. He was brutally honest about his feelings."[9]

When Jesus saw that his friend Lazarus had died, "Jesus wept" even though he knew he would shortly raise Lazarus from the dead (John 11:35). We need to recapture a biblical perspective on the role of emotions in our lives and experience them to the fullest.[10]

When we have been traumatized, hurt, or sinned against, it is appropriate to *feel* the painful impact of what has happened to us. To do otherwise is to deny an essential aspect of being human. We were not designed to act as if our wounds never happened, or to deny them. Nor should we superficially recite Scripture as an incantation to erase our pain. A vital part of spiritual health and emotional maturity is to tend to our wounds. As we appropriately grieve our wounds, sins, and traumas, we will move through a healing process in which our past wounds are integrated into our healthy selves and create a biblically based narrative of our life, just as Paul did. This is the fertile ground of redemption, out of which ministry grows.

HOW TO PROCESS OUR PAINFUL WOUNDS

There are two components to processing your painful experiences in a godly, healthy way. First, allow yourself to process your past painful wounds *emotionally and compassionately* by allowing yourself to feel those emotions that you have suppressed, denied, or have not fully acknowledged. Second, as explained in chapter 17, process your past painful wounds *rationally* through a biblical worldview to gain an understanding of God's perspective and purposes in your specific circumstances. Here, we will examine these separately. In practice, our past must be processed emotionally and rationally at the same time.[11] This is best accomplished in prayer and in a relationship—by telling your story to a trusted friend or counselor who can listen with a compassionate and empathetic presence.[12] Based on the pioneering works of Bessel Van der Kolk, Judith Herman, Diane Langberg, Dan Allender, and others, we know that it is not enough to intellectually and rationally engage your story because our entire nervous system is exquisitely designed to react to trauma; emotional trauma affects and is stored in the whole body and deeply impacts neurophysiological mechanisms.[13] Although an examination of the role of the polyvagal system and trauma is beyond the scope of this book, Van der Kolk explains that the term refers to the branches of the vagus nerve "which connects numerous organs including the brain, lungs, heart, stomach, and intestines . . . and provide[s] us with a more sophisticated understanding of the biology of safety and danger, one based on the subtle interplay between the visceral experiences of our own bodies and the voices and faces of the people around us."[14] It is polyvagal theory that helps us understand why the relational interactions of attunement, a kind, understanding face, soothing tone of voice, being seen, and feeling heard are so important for true healing to occur.[15] We simply cannot ignore the fact that God has hard-wired our brains and bodies to respond physiologically to stress and trauma. Attempts to heal trauma without taking this into account will be incomplete at best and harmful at worst.

PROCESSING PAINFUL EMOTIONS THE WRONG WAY: MASKING AND MEDICATING

How is one to feel painful emotions, especially when we are used to numbing or medicating our pain? Let's contrast two opposite ways of doing this. One of the most common but unhealthy practices we engage in is the act of "masking and medicating," as depicted in figure 3.[16]

Figure 3: Masking and Medicating

As you will see, engaging in this cyclical pattern is a fool's errand—it will mire you in an endless cycle of pain, addictive patterns of behavior, loss of integrity, and isolation, and eventually may result in "flameout"—a term I use for a devastating moral failure that results in disqualification from ministry.

This unhealthy process begins with the presence of an unpleasant or painful emotion we don't like (i.e., pain, sadness, rejection, anger, loneliness). Because painful emotions are difficult, and most of us have been conditioned to avoid feeling them, we react to painful emotions by masking, numbing, or denying the pain. This is often a knee-jerk reaction learned over many years and can be so instinctual you may not be aware of doing it. Masking over pain makes sense. Why wouldn't you try to get away from the discomfort of painful emotions? Who wants to feel lonely, sad, or angry?

After masking or denying the painful feelings, we then move into the next phase of the cycle. We "medicate" our pain to get relief from it. Forms of medication can range from seemingly benign coping mechanisms to sinful and harmful practices, including overwork, overeating, scrolling online, getting lost in movies, engaging in pornography, having sex, or using alcohol or illicit drugs. Although "medicating" can initially feel exhilarating and bring feelings of relief, this is temporary; the pain inevitably returns and will likely deepen. This sets us up for a cycle that will perpetuate itself and can be addictive. Cornelius Plantinga Jr. has astutely observed that "trying to cure distress with the same thing that caused it is typically the mechanism that closes the trap on an addict."[17]

When we medicate our pain with sinful, addictive behaviors, we then necessarily "split" and engage in "image management," where we present an external image (or false self) on the outside while hiding the reality of our condition on the inside. In splitting, we become two-faced or hypocritical (Galatians 2:13) and fail to walk with integrity. This "integrity gap"—the distance between our private and public life—causes further guilt and shame, deepens our pain, and exacerbates the felt need for more "medication." We then wear a mask to hide our form of medication and lack of integrity. The more we engage in this cycle of masking, medicating, and masking, the more we experience distance from God and others, feel powerless over the ways we medicate, and ultimately feel isolated and alone. For the ministry leader who is called to walk in the light with godly character, the risk of being disqualified from ministry grows, depending on the form of medication he or she engages in. This cycle may end up with the leader being disqualified from ministry due to moral failure.

PROCESSING PAINFUL EMOTIONS THE HEALTHY WAY: CULTIVATING INTIMACY WITH CHRIST

In contrast to masking and medicating, a godly, honest, and healthy approach focuses on experiencing our emotions in a safe, empathetic environment and inviting Christ to be with us at the center of our experience, even in our deepest pain and disappointment. The following section outlines sequential steps that can be taken to process emotions. By including a section on repentance, I don't intend to imply either that *having* emotions is sinful or that *processing* our emotions necessarily requires repentance. However, it is often the case that our attempts to avoid feeling emotions involve sinful conduct, as outlined in our discussion above on masking and medicating. If you have tended to engage in sin to avoid or deal with your pain, then you may find the section on repentance helpful. The steps to this are depicted in figure 4.

Grace-Filled Eyes of Christ

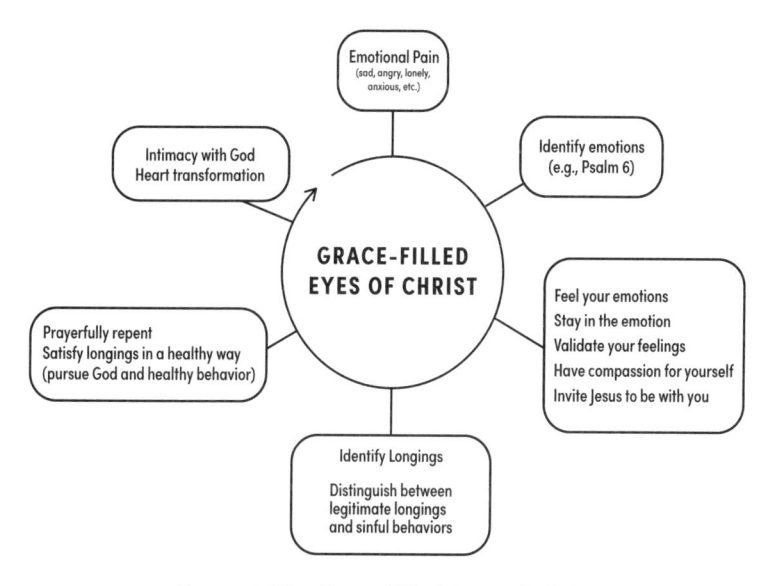

- **Emotional Pain** (sad, angry, lonely, anxious, etc.)
- **Identify emotions** (e.g., Psalm 6)
- Feel your emotions
  - Stay in the emotion
  - Validate your feelings
  - Have compassion for yourself
  - Invite Jesus to be with you
- **Identify Longings**
  - Distinguish between legitimate longings and sinful behaviors
- Prayerfully repent
  - Satisfy longings in a healthy way (pursue God and healthy behavior)
- Intimacy with God
  - Heart transformation

Figure 4: The Grace-Filled Eyes of Christ

Identify and acknowledge your emotions

The process begins the same, with the presence of an unpleasant or painful emotion (i.e., sadness, anger, pain, loneliness). Rather than defaulting to our normal knee-jerk pattern of masking and medicating, we want to *identify* and *acknowledge* the pain without judgment. In the garden of Gethsemane, Jesus "began to be sorrowful and troubled" (Matthew 26:37). Jesus expressly identified and acknowledged these painful emotions when he said, "My soul is very sorrowful, even to death" (v. 38). The Psalms and other Scriptures also model how to do this. As described previously, in Psalm 6 David identifies and acknowledges the range of his deepest emotions to God, honestly expressing his fears, pain, and sadness.

Feel your emotions

The next step is to allow yourself to *feel* your emotions. Ask yourself, "What am I feeling, and where am I feeling it in my body?" God has embodied us as physical beings who feel emotions both in our psyches and our bodies; it is imperative to allow yourself to feel the emotions you are feeling. "We cannot heal what we cannot feel" or "We can reclaim only what we name" are mantras often used by counselors who work with those who grieve or have been traumatized.[18] "You can't heal a wound by saying it's not there!" (Jeremiah 6:14 TLB).

Stay in your emotions

Next, conscientiously and intentionally *stay* in the emotion. This is counterintuitive because everything in us wants to feel better! Because we are so unaccustomed to feeling pain due to habitually masking and medicating, we may be tempted to exit by distracting ourselves, getting busy, or reverting to our usual form of medication. Resist that impulse. Allow yourself to continue to feel what you are feeling. A helpful idea is to *build tolerance* for unpleasant, painful emotions. An apt metaphor for this is stretching one's muscles in preparation for playing sports such as running or skiing. To stretch effectively, we stretch slowly to the point of pain, remain there for a little while, and then relax. When we repeat the stretching exercise, we find we can stretch further and tolerate more pain. Done properly, we gain more flexibility and avoid injury. Similarly, we can build tolerance for experiencing our unpleasant, painful emotions by allowing ourselves to feel and stay in the emotion for a defined period. We can "exit" when we find the pain intolerable, and then enter again when we are ready to reenter the pain.

Validate your emotions

Next, as you acknowledge and feel your emotions, *validate* them without judgment or condemnation. What is validation? When you validate another's emotions, you are providing support and acceptance of his or her emotions, thoughts, and experiences. It does not necessarily mean agreement with the other person's choices or actions. If a client tells me that she is feeling angry, lonely or confused, validation means reflecting empathetically what she is saying in a way that makes her feel heard. It is not the time to try to talk her out of being angry or explain why she "shouldn't" feel what she is feeling. Validating another's experience helps toward healing because it recognizes the person's internal reality, encourages honesty with oneself and others, fosters self-regulation, and normalizes emotions. Interestingly, we often validate another's thoughts, emotions, and experiences but find it difficult to validate our own. In validating our own emotions, we recognize that the emotions we are feeling make sense.

Apply the compassion of Christ

As you validate your emotions without judgment or condemnation, do so with *compassion* and kindness for yourself, just as you might for someone else. This might mean telling yourself, "I'm feeling hurt inside. I'm lonely. It makes sense that I'm feeling this way because . . . (I miss my children, my friend just died, I'm alone on New Year's Eve, etc.)." Validating your emotions with kind compassion is not having a pity party; it is acknowledging the reality of what you are experiencing and not engaging in denial. It is bearing witness to and expressing to yourself the kind, compassionate love that God has for you; it is the kindness of God—not his condemnation—that "leads [us] to repentance" (Romans 2:4). As Dan Allender has eloquently observed, "kindness is the instrument God uses to open the heart and begin its renovation. It is the means God uses to transform fear, hardness, cruelty, and despair. Without kindness, a heart will be bound to the repetition of past trauma in the present."[19] Kindness reflects God's heart toward us and ought to reflect ours as well. Indeed, Scripture describes God as being compassionate and slow to anger and abounding in love and faithfulness at least ten times (e.g., Exodus 66; Numbers 14:18; Joel 2:13).[20]

Consider how Jesus exhibited overwhelming compassion for sinners and outcasts: the leper (Luke 5:12–16), the man possessed by demons (Mark 5:1–8), the woman caught in adultery (John 8:3–11), the prostitute (Luke 7:36–49), the woman with the issue of blood (Mark 5:25–34), the blind (Mark 10:46–52), the Samaritan woman (John 4:7–29), and the thief on the cross (Luke 23:43). Jesus compassionately wept over Jerusalem, the very city "that kills the prophets," saying "How often would I have gathered your children together as a hen gathers her brood under her wings, and you were not willing!" (Luke 13:34; 19:41). Jesus never offered compassion to justify, encourage, or excuse sin; he offered it to provide comfort, healing, and a foundation for repentance. It is good to remind ourselves that Jesus loves us just as he loved each of the sinners he met. Having compassion for yourself is modeling God's character and how Jesus had compassion for himself (Luke 22:39–42) and has compassion for us today. Psychiatrist Curt Thompson has noted how imagining how Jesus views us is part of how our minds are renewed (Romans 12:2): "For our minds to be renewed and formed into the mind of Christ, [we] must practice imagining and then living into the way that Jesus's mind works. . . . This is accomplished only through practice."[21]

Allowing yourself to feel and then compassionately validate your feelings can be particularly challenging if you are used to condemning yourself for having emotions that you believe are not acceptable or you have engaged in shame-inducing behavior. My tendency has been to condemn myself for feeling fearful, doubtful, anxious, or when I struggle with temptation. I tend to scold myself for "being unspiritual" and berate myself for "being weak." But this is precisely what Jesus did *not* do in the garden of Gethsemane when he was in "agony" experiencing the complexity of emotions as he faced his imminent crucifixion (Luke 22:44). He did not condemn himself by saying, "Why are you sweating drops of blood, you are the Son of God, get it together," or "What are you in such agony about, why are you asking God to 'remove this cup' when you know you will be raised from the dead in a few days?" (Luke 22:42). Nor did Jesus engage in spiritual bypass or mask and medicate; he allowed himself to feel his emotions and honestly expressed himself to his Father. Processing our emotions is the time to remind yourself of the gospel and the riches of God's love and grace, which he lavishes on us (Ephesians 1:7–8; 1 John 3:1). Therefore, cultivate the practice of seeing yourself through the compassionate, loving, grace-filled eyes of Jesus, who bore your sins and died for you *precisely because he loves you* and has compassion for you. Imagining what Mary Magdalene experienced as she encountered Jesus, Brennan Manning gives us a taste of Jesus's compassionate love:

> Magdalene was awed by the loveliness and compassion of this magnetic man. His eyes had called out to her, Come to me. Come now. Don't wait until you have your act cleaned up and your head on straight. Don't delay until you think you are properly disposed and free of pride and lust, jealousy and self-hatred. Come to me in your brokenness and sinfulness with your fears and insecurities and I will comfort you. I will come to you right where you

are and love you just the way you are . . . and not the way you think you should be. . . . The creative power of Jesus' love called Magdalene to regard herself as He did, to see in herself the possibilities which he saw in her.[22]

This is how we ought to envision how Jesus sees us and invites us to see ourselves, without self-hatred, self-condemnation, or self-loathing. As Jesus had compassion for the woman caught in adultery and treated her with tender kindness, we ought to have compassion for ourselves (John 8:11).

Invite Jesus Christ to be with you

As you allow yourself to feel your emotions, *invite Christ to be with you* in your pain. Of course, he has been with you during this entire exercise, but if you have been staying in the emotion and not distracting yourself, this is the time when you especially need Christ's presence. Prayerfully express what you are feeling and thinking and invite Jesus to be with you, to comfort you, and to sustain you. In the garden of Gethsemane, Jesus spent the entire evening in deep and intense prayer in the presence of his heavenly father and intimately expressed his feelings and thoughts to God (Matthew 26:37–45). Indeed, Scripture tells us that his body reacted to his emotions by sweating drops of blood. He needed God's strength and power to do what God had called him to do.

As you engage with the Father in prayer while you are experiencing your emotions, you will cultivate intimacy with God who knows your suffering and knows what you desire in that moment.

The decision to allow yourself to feel pain and to invite Christ to be with you in your pain is a key factor in engaging in active repentance by breaking the cycle of masking and medicating. If you've habitually medicated when you've felt pain, you will instinctively want to medicate again; if you have engaged in addictive forms of medication such as alcohol, pornography, or drugs, it will be much harder to break that cycle due to the impact of the brain chemistry that is activated when we engage in certain addictive behaviors.[23] The urge to medicate will likely increase. That is normal and expected; continue to resist.

Identify your longings

At this point, it is very helpful to *identify what you are longing for* in that moment. When we medicate, we are trying to satisfy a deep longing within. Many of us are not in touch with what we deeply long for in those moments. For example, we may superficially conclude that the desire to look at pornography may be a desire for sex, but there are much deeper longings that are motivating the desire for pornography.[24] Beneath the urge to look at porn can be a more profound desire for intimacy, to be known, to be loved, to have impact, or to exercise control, to name a few. It is crucial to make the distinction between *what* you are longing for and the *way* you are trying to *fulfill* that longing. Your longing may be godly, but you may be engaging in sinful conduct to fulfill that longing. Many make the mistake of trying to repent of godly longings when repentance from sinful behavior is what is necessary.

Understanding our longings *under* our longings is also crucial for not being controlled by our desires and restoring the ability to make choices to not engage in sinful conduct. The degree to which you are not in touch with the motivations and longings of your heart is the degree to which your behavior will feel more compulsive and over which you have no control. Conversely, the degree to which you get in touch with your longings is the degree to which your behavior will feel less compulsive, and you will begin to be able to exercise volition over your behavior.[25] In other words, rather than focusing on controlling sinful behavior that feels compulsive, ask yourself, "What am I longing for right now?" Often, you will begin to see that what you are longing for is *not* the behavior you are engaging in but something much deeper, understandable, godly, and good. Identifying the *longing under the longing* often removes the compulsive feelings and desires to engage in sinful behavior; when we do so, we can go to God to fulfill the deeper, more profound longing that no sinful behavior can fulfill. As you resist the temptation to numb, exit, or medicate, you will gain more control over your behavior and have an increased ability to exercise your will to not engage in that behavior.

As an illustration, let's consider the bitter jealousy that Joseph's brothers experienced when their father favored Joseph and examine their longings (Genesis 37:3). If you had been able to counsel Joseph's brothers as they conspired to kill him and asked them to identify their longings, they initially would have said, "We hate Joseph and want him dead" (see Genesis 37:18). If you had further asked them to pause and reflect on what they *really* longed for, they could have identified the longing *under* the longing: their father's love. The apparent desire to kill Joseph was deeply sinful; the *longing under* that desire to experience their father's affectionate love was good and godly. Suppose you suggested that if they engaged in the sinful conduct of murdering (or selling) Joseph, they still would not have received what they deeply longed for. That would have given them an opportunity to (1) identify their more profound longings under the immediate desire to kill Joseph, (2) think about the consequences of sinning against Joseph, (3) understand that sinning against Joseph would not get them what they truly longed for, (4) not take action to sin against Joseph, and (5) develop godly strategies to get what they truly longed for—their father's love. Indeed, by selling Joseph and lying about his death (Genesis 37:30–33), Joseph's brothers never experienced the love from their father that they desired. What would it mean to you if you were able to stop masking and medicating by feeling your pain and then explore the longings under your longings, thereby restoring your volition to choose to pursue God and godly behavior?

Prayerfully repent

At this juncture, if applicable, you will find it helpful to repent by explicitly acknowledging how you previously processed your pain and prayerfully ask God to help you turn away from whatever you have used to avoid or medicate your painful emotions. Thus, the process of engaging with God *as you experience your pain* will have the important benefit of helping you repent of the specific thing you previously used to medicate.

Here is an example of what it may look like to integrate processing your emotions with a prayer of repentance from sinful forms of medication:

> Father, I acknowledge that I'm feeling lonely right now. I feel that loneliness in my chest, and it feels like there is a hole there—and a deep ache. Please be with me as I allow myself to feel these unpleasant sensations and help me to tolerate this pain rather than exiting from it—even for a few minutes. I acknowledge that I'm accustomed to medicating this lonely feeling by (e.g., working long hours, using pornography, overeating, scrolling, manipulating others, or staying busy) and I have created an idol out of this form of medication rather than going to you, the fountain of living waters. Like the children of Israel,

I dig cisterns that can hold no water (Jeremiah 2:13). I see the futility of this behavior and my lack of power over it.

I ask you to help me repent and stay here with you in your presence. I thank you for having born this sin and making me righteous through the blood of Jesus. There is now no condemnation because I am in Jesus (Romans 8:1). I am beginning to see that I have turned to my form of medication (e.g., pornography, overeating, overworking) because deep inside, I am really longing for (relief, power, control, affirmation, comfort, admiration, to be known, to be seen, to have impact, to be married, etc.). I'm turning to you to fill me and fulfill my longings. I pray that you would fill me now and help me to get my longings filled in legitimate ways rather than by turning to sinful strategies.

Pursue God and healthy behavior

Finally, as you turn from masking and medicating, think about how you can *satisfy your longings by pursuing God and engaging in godly, healthy behavior.* Perhaps you have experienced God's miraculous presence and comfort in moments of deep pain. Sometimes, when we ask God to intervene in our lives, he answers with a wonderful feeling of peace and presence that gives immediate relief. There have been times when God has come through for me in that way. Often, however, he does not immediately answer our prayers in the way we want; we may continue to feel painful emotions and not get the immediate relief we desire. Either way, we can exercise our volition to seek God and choose godly behavior rather than medicating. For example, rather than medicating loneliness with pornography, we can cultivate healthy friendships and grow deeper community. Rather than medicating anxiety by getting drunk, we can seek out a wise counselor. Whether we feel immediate comfort and relief or continue to be in pain, we can trust that God is in control of our lives and that, over time, he is working in our hearts to *develop our character and our intimacy with him through the sanctification process* (James 1:2).

Processing your emotions this way will likely be a new and helpful experience for you. It will take time to develop but will eventually become a fruitful godly discipline for you. Use figure 4 as a spiritual discipline, and over time, engaging in this process will become habitual and replace your previous habit of self-medicating. Processing your emotions with God will allow you to address your wounds and bring healing to your heart. You will then be more ready to move to the next step, allowing God to redeem your wounds by applying biblical truth to your experiences to help you see God's purposes and provisions for you.

REFLECTION QUESTIONS

1. What did you learn about emotions in your family of origin? What were some of the messages you received from your family and your church about how to handle or express emotion?
2. How do you "medicate" your pain, and what are the specific triggers that make it likely you will medicate?
3. How does medicating your pain affect your relationship with God, your spouse, your children, your friends, or your church?
4. When you consider validating your own emotions without judgment and with compassion, what thoughts and feelings come up for you? Do you find yourself resisting this? Why?
5. Read the narrative of Jesus's experience in the garden of Gethsemane (Matthew 26). List all the emotions he experienced. How did he handle them? What lessons can you learn from the way Jesus handled his emotions?

6. Take one painful memory and engage in healthy emotional processing by working through each of the steps in figure 4 on page 151.

Chapter 16
LET CHRIST BE OUR STRENGTH

The fourth step in addressing our ruling passions is to *embrace our weaknesses* and revel in the radical biblical truth that when we are weak, Christ is strong in us (2 Corinthians 12:8–10). This is counterintuitive and countercultural, turning our natural tendency to emphasize our strengths upside down. When we remember the experiences and feel the emotional pain out of which our ruling passions developed, we will likely find the vows that we made to be a defensive response to feelings of vulnerability and weakness. None of us want to feel the shame associated with weakness. Yet, reflecting on the wounds and weaknesses that were foundational to developing our ruling passions can help us see our weaknesses as the very place where we can experience the power and strength of Christ, becoming fully dependent on him, not ourselves. Thus, we can allow our weaknesses, and the painful events in our lives, to turn us *toward* God, our Redeemer, who transforms our weaknesses into strength for his glory.

We've already examined how the apostle Paul experienced dozens of traumatic events and was often miraculously delivered from dire circumstances. However, there were times when God did *not* answer his prayers in the way he wanted, and he suffered as a result. In writing to the Corinthian church, Paul described a time when God did not relieve him of what he described as a "thorn in the flesh" (2 Corinthians 12:7). Although the Bible does not identify Paul's thorn, it was deeply distressing to him, and Paul prayed fervently and repeatedly for God to remove it. Yet God did not. Paul described how God met him in this place of weakness and altered his view of the thorn into something deeply transformative:

> Three times I pleaded with the Lord about this, that it should leave me. But he said to me, "My grace is sufficient for you, for my power is made perfect in weakness." Therefore I will boast all the more gladly of my weaknesses, so that the power of Christ may rest upon me. For the sake of Christ, then, I am content with weaknesses, insults, hardships, persecutions, and calamities. For when I am weak, then I am strong. (2 Corinthians 12:8–10)

Rather than denying or running from his weaknesses, Paul realized they played three important functions in his life. First, experiencing weakness kept Paul from "becoming conceited" (2 Corinthians 12:7). Paul understood that given his miraculous conversion, heavenly vision (2 Corinthians 12:1–6) and large impact as he shared the gospel and planted multiple churches, he had a tendency toward pride. The thorn helped him remain humble even as he became increasingly influential.

Second, the thorn fostered a dependence on Christ's sovereign power rather than his own.[1] There is a tendency when we experience success, particularly in ministry, to take credit for it or to attribute the success to our own gifts and skills. Understanding that the true source of his ministry success rested in *Christ's power* kept Paul balanced and truly dependent on Christ.

Finally, the thorn created a strength in Paul that was based on Christ's strength. It was in that place of humility and weakness that Paul was able to proclaim, "I can do all things through him who strengthens me," and be fueled to engage in powerful, effective ministry as he served God (Philippians 4:13).

How can we apply these truths to our lives? Many spend a lifetime trying to distance themselves from weaknesses. We deny, hide, or cover up. We compensate for shame by pouring our energies into developing areas of strength and competence, which we wear like masks, creating a false self. This is dishonest and exhausting. In a radical upside-down statement, Paul's solution was to boast of his weaknesses, accepting and embracing them. In doing this, he allowed room for the true strength of Christ to flow through him.

Admitting our weaknesses is especially liberating when we feel shame over them. Shame is like a dark monster, sucking the air out of a room. The strategy of hiding something in shame doesn't work and ultimately steals our effectiveness.

I have many weaknesses. I have suffered from anxiety and a bad case of insecurity most of my life. One of my weaknesses is that I have engaged in a practice that I suspect many ministry leaders engage in: I have compared myself to others whom I perceive as smarter and better communicators than me.

I have seen speakers able to recall great volumes of information without looking at notes, and spontaneously access factual content as if they were reading from a book. In the past, when I was around a speaker or preacher who made me feel inferior, my initial response was to develop a judgmental spirit, criticizing some aspect of his presentation. Deep inside, however, I was envious. At first, my envy was unconscious. I was only slightly aware of judging him or not liking him.

Over time, I began to be vaguely conscious of my envy, but then I felt shame for being envious. The idea of being envious was so unacceptable to me that I buried it and had much difficulty in acknowledging my envy to myself, much less others. I would also condemn myself for not being smart, competent, or skilled enough. The negative thoughts (lies) in my head went something like this: "You are so stupid and incompetent; if you were smart you would remember those details and you would not have to look at your notes. That speaker is so much smarter, so much more competent. You have nothing to offer when you teach. You might as well quit." As you can imagine, struggling with these negative thoughts brought on more shame, discouragement, and anxiety. You can see my trajectory: my natural inclination was to think how inferior I was to others, which led to being envious of others, which then led to shame, self-condemnation, and frustration for feeling this way in the first place.

When I began to take seriously Paul's experience of finding strength in weakness, it was helpful and liberating. I learned to be honest with myself about my insecurities, anxieties, and envious thoughts. Rather than denying my weaknesses, I admitted them to God and myself. Rather than comparing myself to others and condemning myself, I began to allow myself to feel the pain caused by my perceived weaknesses and think truthfully about them and myself. Because I know God loves, accepts, and even delights over me, I can go to him in honest prayer. Here's what that sounds like:

> God, I long to be a good speaker, to have something to offer, and really wish I could speak like Pete. I wish I were able to remember details like he can. However, I recognize that you have given him certain gifts and callings, and you have given me different gifts and callings. I also

recognize that my learning style is different from his, and my ability to remember is not like his. Pete has a much better memory than me and that's ok. I recognize that my inability to remember is a weakness that I have, and my underlying insecurity is an even greater weakness.

Would you help me where I am weak? Would you be strong for me in my weakness? Would you help me deal with my feelings of insecurity and help me be strong in you? Would you help me to not be envious of Pete, but to rejoice in the gifts that you have given him? Would you help me be content with the abilities, skills, strengths, gifts, and callings that you have given me? Help me to depend on your strength and trust that you will use me in accordance with your will and your power, not mine. I recognize that when I am weak you are strong.

Just the act of praying in this way relieves shame and guilt. It is *redemptive* because my negative, self-condemning thoughts are seen for what they are in the presence of my loving, grace-filled Savior who already knows me and loves me as I am. No longer do these shame-filled thoughts have the same power over me. As I let these parts of myself be seen by God, myself, and others, I'm able to think more accurately about the thoughts and feelings I experience. Now instead of saying, "I *am* incompetent," I can say, "I may *feel* incompetent, but God is my strength, and when I'm weak and feeling incompetent, then I am strong in him." The distinction between *being* incompetent and *feeling* incompetent is seismic.

There often is a huge difference between our feelings and reality. My feelings are fickle and often tied to an ingrained negative lens that keeps me from accurately perceiving myself and others. And even when I correctly see myself as weak, I can rely on God—God sees me and loves me even when I *am* weak, and he will perform what he wants through me, despite my own perceived and actual weaknesses. With Paul, I can say honestly, "For the sake of Christ, then, I am content with weaknesses.... For when I am weak, then I am strong" (2 Corinthians 12:10).

As you reflect on your feelings of weakness and vulnerability, take them directly to God in prayer and allow him to be your strength.

REFLECTION QUESTIONS

1. Are there areas in your life that you see as analogous to Paul's "thorn in the flesh"? What are they?
2. What fears or obstacles do you encounter as you contemplate admitting your weaknesses to yourself or others? What might happen if you honestly assessed and admitted your weaknesses?
3. What positive impact might you have on others in allowing them to see areas where you are weak, incompetent, or insecure?
4. Can you identify an example in your life where you initially failed at something (e.g., relational failure, an attempt at a new skill, sports) but that failure ultimately became the basis for succeeding?
5. Compose a prayer that is like the prayer on pages 166-67. Express yourself honestly to God about your weaknesses, longings, and fears.

Chapter 17
WALK IN THE TRUTH

A.W. Tozer said, "What comes into our minds when we think about God is the most important thing about us."[1] Another important thing about us is what comes into our minds when we think about ourselves, and whether our thinking is grounded in the truth. Every ruling passion, at its foundation, has beliefs we have developed about God, ourselves, and the world. The fifth step in biblically responding to our ruling passions is to walk in the truth, wisely applying it to our hearts.

The apostle Paul instructed, "Do not be conformed to this world, but be transformed by the renewal of your mind, that by testing you may discern what is the will of God, what is good and acceptable and perfect" (Romans 12:2). Transformation involves renewing our minds, and an essential element of this renewal is knowing and walking in the truth. The fundamental question we must ask ourselves is whether what we believe (about anything and everything) is true or false. The process of transformation begins by asking this question specifically about our interpretations of our experiences and the beliefs we carry and then comparing them to both biblical truth and general revelation. As psychiatrist Timothy Jennings observed, the "truth is only beneficial when it is understood, believed and applied."[2]

There is a wide range of false beliefs that we can carry—beliefs about ourselves (e.g., "I'm too old to learn a musical instrument," "If I make a mistake, I must be a total failure," "I fail at everything I do"), other people (e.g., "no one likes me," "people think I'm dumb"), God (e.g., "God allowed that trauma because he despises me," "God helps those who help themselves"), and other categories. Our beliefs can be conscious or unconscious, held loosely or tightly, and we can be highly resistant to changing our beliefs, depending on many factors, including their origin and our experiences. Many beliefs are developed early in life and can form the core of an individual's self-concept.[3] Other beliefs are formed as we develop and are based on conclusions we draw from relationships and life experiences.

Importantly, our false beliefs can have many negative consequences: they can impact our view of self, hinder our ability to live by the truth revealed in Scripture, and prevent us from seeing God and the world accurately. False beliefs can be the genesis of anxiety and depression and can stop us from living productive, healthy, satisfying lives.[4] False beliefs can prevent us from experiencing the sanctifying work of the Holy Spirit. Unfortunately, many destructive false beliefs are frequently cloaked in, or resemble most closely, an important truth about God, ourselves, and the world, but have been distorted in ways to which we can be blind.

EXAMINE THE MEANING YOU ASCRIBED TO YOUR EXPERIENCES

A crucial aspect of walking in the truth is accurately interpreting our past and present experiences. God is rational, and the world he created is based, in part, on the laws of reason and logic—laws that he invented. We are meaning makers—that is, we too are designed to think logically and rationally, to ascribe accurate meaning to and draw conclusions from the circumstances and events in our lives.[5] We all ascribe meaning to our past experiences to make sense of them. When we remember painful experiences, we often assume that it is the experience itself that was so painful. However, it is not the experience itself, but *the meaning* ascribed to the event that makes the memory so painful. It is that meaning that creates the soil from which our ruling passions grow and informs how we will live our lives. And the meaning we ascribe to our experiences may be accurate or inaccurate.

For example, being rejected can be a painful memory. But it is not the rejection itself that hurts so much. It is both the *memory* of being rejected and the *meaning* ascribed to that particular experience of being rejected that is so painful. Take, for example, a woman who went through the painful experience of being rejected by her father as a six-year-old girl when he left her and her mother to have an adulterous affair. At the time, she did not know about her father's relationship with the other woman. Given her limited understanding of the facts, and her limited cognitive ability as a child, she erroneously believed he left because he had been displeased by her. In her childlike mind, she reasoned, "He left me because I was not a good daughter." It is common for children to blame themselves for others' bad behavior even when they have no actual responsibility for that behavior.[6]

Was it the *fact* of her father leaving or the *meaning she ascribed to why* her father left that led her to create the vow to never be rejected again? Her father's behavior had nothing to do with her; she bore no responsibility for her father leaving to have an affair. Her interpretation of that past painful event was false. Children of tender years do not have the knowledge, cognitive ability, or emotional maturity to accurately interpret the facts or cope with the pain of rejection. Part of her healing journey involves looking back on her experiences through a biblical lens. As an adult she has other resources—including the Word of God, her relationship with the Lord, her relationships with other healthy friends, and her ability to engage in accurate, rational thinking about her interpretations of the past—to help her overcome her ruling passion to not be rejected. And as she no longer is ruled by her fears of being rejected, she will be able to enter deeper, more authentic relationships.

Two people can go through virtually identical experiences and ascribe completely different meanings to them. Two pastors preach brilliant, well-delivered sermons and both receive a critical comment from a congregant. Pastor Jones may easily disregard the comment ascribing the accurate meaning that the congregant is immature and does not value biblical teaching; Pastor Smith may feel wounded and depressed as a result, ascribing the inaccurate meaning that the congregant's comment represented most of the congregation's opinion about his preaching ability.

We have a choice regarding how we view our past experiences. Slowing down and intentionally seeing our past through a biblical lens is fundamental to and essential for transformation.

SEE GOD'S SOVEREIGN PLAN AND PROVIDENTIAL HAND IN YOUR LIFE

Walking in the truth means seeing the sovereign hand of God in our lives, especially when our experiences are difficult and painful. One of the most challenging and yet profound and liberating truths I have heard is this: "You have the exact past God wants (or allowed) you to have. You can't change your past, but you can be a good steward of your past and use it for his glory!"[7] God is sovereign; he was and is in control of all things. Nothing happens apart from his divine plan. Nothing happens by accident. And God can take our tragedies, pain, hurts, losses, and even abuse and redeem them for his glory.

The concept of God's sovereignty and his control over the details of one's life is understandably difficult to comprehend, especially for those who have suffered loss, abuse, trauma, and tragedy. Although a detailed treatment of this subject is beyond the scope of this book, it is helpful to realize that the most tragic, cruel, and horrendous crime of the universe, the crucifixion of God's Son, was explicitly planned and intended by God. Peter and John saw God's sovereign hand at work in Jesus's crucifixion. Peter states,

> "Men of Israel, hear these words: Jesus of Nazareth, a man attested to you by God with mighty works and wonders and signs that God did through him in your midst, as you yourselves know— *this Jesus, delivered up according to the definite plan and foreknowledge of God*, you crucified and killed by the hands of lawless men. God raised him up, loosing the pangs of death, because it was not possible for him to be held by it." (Acts 2:22–24)

Note that the passage includes both that Jesus was killed according to the "definite plan and foreknowledge of God" and at the same time, God holds those who killed him responsible, calling them "lawless men."

Further, in Acts 4, the apostles Peter and John, while addressing God in prayer, state, "for truly in this city there were gathered together against your holy servant Jesus, whom you anointed, both Herod and Pontius Pilate, along with the Gentiles and the peoples of Israel, *to do whatever your hand and your plan had predestined to take place*" (Acts 4:27–28).[8]

JOSEPH'S ABUSE AND GOD'S SOVEREIGNTY

It is hard to find a narrative that more clearly lays out God's sovereignty than the story of Joseph. Joseph was treated brutally by his brothers. They stripped and beat him and sold him to slave traders who, in turn, sold him to an Egyptian officer (Genesis 37–50). As a result of his brothers' abuse, Joseph spent decades separated from his beloved father and his family and endured harsh treatment at the hands of the Egyptians. He was falsely accused of attempted rape and imprisoned unjustly, left to languish in prison for years. Despite his troubles, Joseph remained faithful to God and sought to honor him even when he was victimized over many years in difficult circumstances.

In Genesis 45 we see how, in an incredible way, God's sovereign control over everything accomplished God's purposes through suffering. Through a series of events orchestrated by God's providential hand, Joseph eventually became second-in-command of the Egyptian government, and Joseph's brothers ended up standing before Joseph. Given his position of power and his brothers' grievous sins against him, Joseph could easily have exacted revenge on them. Rather than using his memories of his past wounds to justify disobeying God and taking revenge, he tells his brothers,

> "And now do not be . . . angry with yourselves because you sold me here, *for God sent me before you to preserve life*. For the famine has been in the land these two years, and there are yet five years in which there will be neither plowing nor harvest. *And God sent me* before you to preserve for you a remnant on earth, and to keep alive for you many survivors. *So it was not you who sent me here, but God.*" (Genesis 45:5–8)

Joseph's behavior and the meaning that he ascribed to the horrendous treatment he received at the hands of his brothers are stunning, especially given the fact that he lived in a Middle Eastern culture that valued revenge against those who betrayed one's family. But Joseph viewed his past and present through the accurate lens of God's sovereignty and used his past as an *opportunity* to minister to his own immediate family and the entire nation of Egypt.

There are two significant lessons we can learn from Joseph as we ask God to redeem our ruling passions by walking in the truth. First, Joseph saw God's sovereign reign and providential hand at work, *even in the evil acts committed by his brothers*. He says, "God sent me before you to preserve [life]," and later, even more explicitly, he says: "*So it was not you who sent me here, but God.*" That last statement ought to stop us in our tracks. Even though his brothers beat and sold him, Joseph understood that it was God's unseen hand orchestrating these acts. Although Joseph could not have known it at the time he was beaten, enslaved, and thrown into prison, God was working his purposes through those painful circumstances to save the nation of Israel, "the remnant" out of which was born our Savior, Jesus

Christ. God redeemed Joseph's past, his abuse, and his pain and carried out his purpose through him. Tim Keller makes this observation about Joseph:

> Standing where we do, we can look back and ask whether God was really "missing in action" all of those years when he seemed to be absent from Joseph's life. When Joseph prayed for his life in that cistern, did God really not hear him? And all those years when absolutely everything seemed to go wrong for Joseph, was God not there? No, he was there, and he was working. He was hidden, but he was also in complete control.⁹

Joseph recognized that God was present, and he used the memories of trauma and abuse to embrace the truth that *God is always in control, orchestrating events, including our suffering, for his unseen, greater purposes.* Although his brothers engaged in despicable, evil acts against him and caused him incredible suffering, Joseph extended grace to them. This is evidence that Joseph's ruling passions were godly. Are you able to look at the past and present circumstances of your life and see God's hidden hand and purposes?

Second, although Joseph endured terrible injustices against him, he did not ascribe negative or inaccurate meanings to those incidents. At key points in his life, Joseph could have interpreted his older brothers' brutal treatment, being unjustly accused of rape, or being thrown in prison as meaning that he was a loser, destined for failure, or that God was against him. Such interpretations would have been inaccurate. Had he accepted such misinterpretations of his experiences, he might have walked a different path that was self-destructive and full of revenge. Joseph allowed his memories of painful experiences and the accurate meaning he made of those experiences to be redemptive in his life. Joseph's decision impacted his life, the life of his immediate family, the nation of Egypt, and the lives of generations of Israelites who followed him (Genesis 50:20).

GOD'S PURPOSES PREVAIL EVEN IN OUR SUFFERING

A modern example of someone who has viewed traumatic events in her life through the lens of God's sovereignty is Joni Eareckson Tada, who was tragically paralyzed after a diving accident. Joni echoed this biblical concept saying, "God will permit what he hates to accomplish that which he loves."[10] This truth provided Joni with assurance that God despises suffering. Jesus spent much of his time relieving people of suffering, but because we live in a fallen world, God allows his people to suffer to "accomplish what he loves." She explains:

> In this wheelchair, I know that suffering has made my faith more muscular . . . has deepened my prayer life, made me more interested in the Bible, and . . . helped me learn patience and endurance. I know that my suffering has made heaven come alive . . . made me more sensitive to others who hurt. Most of all, it has helped me to identify with Jesus in His suffering; it has helped me grasp a tiny little inkling of all the awful things Jesus went through to secure my salvation. . . . And when problems for me pile on even higher—like chronic pain and cancer on top of quadriplegia—then it drives me even deeper into the arms of Jesus. And this is what God loves to accomplish in our lives, and He uses our hardships and pain and problems to do.[11]

Understanding our experiences through the providential lens of God's redemptive purposes is an essential key to healing and transforming our ruling passions. While it is difficult to reconcile the concept of a God who is good and loving with the unspeakable tragedies that many endure in this life, I'm convinced that in God's timing we will see all events through God's perspective of eternity. Commenting that Psalm 39 expresses terrible pain without any hope, Tim Keller came to a startling but insightful conclusion:

> It is remarkable that God not only allows his creatures to complain to him of their ills but *actually records those wails in his Word*. "The very presence of such prayers in Scripture is a witness to His understanding. He knows how men speak when they are desperate." *God is confident we will look back at that and close our mouths, lost in wonder at the spectacular love that planned even our darkest moments.*[12]

MY HEARTBREAK: THE WORST THING REDEEMED FOR THE BEST THING

On a more personal note, when I was twenty-four years old, I experienced the painful breakup of my first marriage when my wife left me. Curt Thompson has observed that suffering not only arises from relational injuries we experience but also from *our responses to those injuries*.[13] My response to this injury can be seen in the inaccurate meanings I ascribed to my divorce which encompassed a constellation of negative beliefs that included "I'm defective," "I have nothing to offer," "I'm a loser," "I'm not lovable," and "I'll be rejected if I allow someone to know me." For years, I used these negative meanings to justify disobeying God, harden my heart, and justify sinful behavior. I serve myself by engaging in a series of relationships with women in which, frankly, I became a "consumer." As explained more fully in chapter 19, seeking relief from the pain of loneliness was my ruling passion.

Over time, however, I realized that although my self-protective behavior served as a temporary anesthetic, it also prevented me from receiving love and loving others unconditionally the way God intended. I can see now that God was allowing what he hated—rejection, abandonment, divorce—to accomplish what he loves: softening my heart, creating empathy for others, and cultivating an attitude willing to be committed to loving others. I have tried to be a good steward of my painful past by using the memories of my painful experiences to increase my love for God and others. Now, looking back, I can see God's providential hand in redeeming such a painful experience by serving many people who have been abandoned and rejected. If I had not been through that pain, I would not be able to empathize with them, to help them, or to have a vision for their future. I believe that God has given a lot of people hope by allowing that difficult time in my life.

REPLACING FALSE BELIEFS WITH THE TRUTH

We have spent a good deal of time discussing how to see our past through the biblical lens of God's sovereignty. How are we to apply the truth to our hearts to squarely address the false beliefs that we carry with us? A helpful analysis is to (1) identify our false beliefs and comprehend *why* they are false, and (2) replace the false beliefs with the truth. This is in line with Paul's admonition to "take every thought captive" to Christ (2 Corinthians 10:5). Let's now look at an example to see how this works by examining how Pastor Jack was able to identify his false beliefs and walk in the truth in a difficult situation at his church.

Pastor Jack's false beliefs about leadership

Pastor Jack has been serving as the solo pastor in a small country church in the US for nearly twenty years. Jack sought help because he found that he was ineffective in leading his congregation, saying that people did not respond well to or respect his leadership. He noted that his congregants viewed him as "nice, but spineless and incompetent." Compounding the problem, his failure to exercise balanced, strong leadership caused others who wielded stronger personalities to usurp his authority and exert their will on issues. This had a detrimental effect on the church.

Let's examine how his ruling passions were born out of his earlier experiences and how his false beliefs about leadership had a negative impact on his ability to lead his church well.

Jack's father was a pastor with a domineering personality. Angry, gruff, and demanding, he ruled both his home and church with a heavy hand. His father often made scenes in public by being rude and often offended his congregants. Jack felt embarrassed and ashamed of him and vowed to "never be like him." Jack developed the underlying beliefs that being strong and forceful in leadership would hurt those around him, and that to be a successful Pastor Jack would have to be "caring, nice, and never impose" himself on others. He further believed that if he were to "lead with strength," he would turn people off and lose their respect. As a result, he made the following silent, unconscious vow to himself: "I will always be caring, I will never hurt or impose my will on others." As he reflected on his years of pastoral ministry, here is how Jack described how that vow manifested itself as he exercised leadership in his congregation:

> When I lead meetings I try hard to not impose my opinion on others; I am deferential by default. I take a back seat and am careful to not offend others. I avoid contradicting others whose opinions are different from mine because I don't want to hurt their feelings, even to the point of nodding my head when I disagree with them. This often gives the impression that I agree with what they are saying when I don't. I am uncomfortable when someone expresses his opinion forcefully and usually remain quiet. I believe that I don't have much to offer and that I'll be an inconvenience and bother others when I offer my opinion. When I'm honest with myself, I believe that I am incompetent. I'm not the leader that I have been called to be.

Ironically, Jack's legitimate longings to lead well, not hurt others, and be respected as a competent pastor were undermined by his weak leadership style that had the opposite effect: others usurped his authority, caused harm to congregants, and disrespected Jack.

Here are some of the steps we took to address Jack's leadership dilemma. First, we began by recognizing Jack's legitimate longing to be a competent pastor. He desired to treat others with respect and to avoid being a domineering, offensive, and abusive leader. These were good goals. I reminded him that when we take a good thing and make it an ultimate thing, it then becomes an idol.

Second, Jack then identified and articulated the web of false beliefs (lies) that were embedded in his thought processes and the way he exercised leadership. Before working with me, he had never expressed his beliefs clearly; they had remained vague and undefined. Here is how Jack articulated his false beliefs more clearly:

- "Being strong and forceful in leadership will hurt others."
- "If I lead with strength people will not respect me."
- "Being successful means I must never impose myself or my opinions on others."
- "My thoughts and opinions are an inconvenience to my congregants."

Third, Jack began to ascertain *why* these beliefs were false. I encouraged him to test the truth or falsity of his beliefs by asking the following life-changing questions:

- Is the belief (always) *true*?
- What is the *evidence* for my belief?
- What *false assumptions* am I making?

As an example, we addressed Jack's belief that "being strong and forceful in leadership will hurt others" by asking whether that is always true, or are there times when being strong and forceful will help others? As he reflected on his experience, he could not give any examples of his decisions hurting others. To the contrary, he was able to identify many examples where being decisive had helped people in his congregation and where people were *relieved* that he had been decisive.

Jack also identified some false assumptions embedded in his beliefs. He had falsely assumed that "being strong and forceful in leadership" equated with being rude or acting in a dominating manner (as his father had). He had incorrectly assumed that strong leadership and gentle shepherding were mutually exclusive. Somehow in twenty years of pastoring he had failed to see how he had unconsciously fused the concept of strong leadership with abusive leadership. He also provided examples where he or others had made good decisions and communicated them in a gentle, kind manner, thus highlighting the false assumption in his belief.

Replacing Jack's false beliefs with the truth

As Jack examined the false assumptions embedded in his beliefs, he realized that there are instances where authoritative, decisive leadership is loving, is helpful, and can be provided in a gentle manner. Jack had to replace the false beliefs with the truths. Here is a sample of how Jack was able to do this:

- "Being strong and forceful in leadership will hurt others" was reframed and replaced with the truth that "good leaders can be gentle and strong while being assertive; when I lead with the appropriate balance of strength, I will be serving the church and will prevent others from being hurt."
- "If I lead with strength people will not respect me" was reframed and replaced with the truth that "As the pastor, God has called me to lead with Christlike strength, and when I lead this way it is likely that people will respect me. However, whether I'm respected is not as important as leading in the way God wants me to, and the most important value is to love my congregation by leading gently as God gives me wisdom."
- "Being successful means I must never impose myself on others" was reframed and replaced with the truth that "sometimes I must assert myself in ways that are difficult for me and may cause others to disagree with me. It is understandable that I feel uncomfortable given the negative behavior modeled by my father. Loving and leading well sometimes means I will feel uncomfortable, and that

people may disagree with my decision. I'm not called to be successful but faithful."

- "My thoughts and opinions are an inconvenience to my congregants" was reframed and replaced with the truth that "It is biblical that I am not to think more highly of myself than I ought, and I know that my thoughts and opinions are not infallible, but God has given me a good mind and I am able to exercise wise judgment as I seek God and the counsel of others. Therefore, my thoughts and opinions matter and are good for my congregants."

Although it may seem laborious to engage each of the false beliefs in the manner outlined above, this is an essential exercise; we must thoroughly challenge and refute the false beliefs that we carry to be freed from the tyranny they hold over us. We must create a rhythm and habit of reflection on and reorientation of these underlying beliefs and replace them with the truth. It may feel uncomfortable at first, but as you regularly engage in the process of replacing false beliefs with the truth, it will become an easier and habitual process that develops the instincts of walking in the truth. This exercise helped Jack to become more nuanced about his leadership. As he adopted and walked in the truth with his congregation, he began to exercise godly competent leadership and began to regain the respect of his congregation.

We are called to know and walk in the truth in every area of our lives, including biblical doctrine and the narratives and beliefs by which we live our lives. Our false beliefs can have significant and long-term consequences. They can wreak havoc on our emotional lives by creating anxiety and depression, limit the choices that we make, hinder our ability to move out in our world, and inhibit our willingness to live out our calling. When we courageously refute them, it changes our lives. Had Pastor Jack left his false beliefs unexamined and unchallenged, his leadership would have remained severely compromised.

Believing and applying truth to our hearts is not as simple as it sounds. It is not what we *think* we believe but what we *actually* believe that has the most profound impact on our lives. It is possible to be an expert in theology and doctrine, to be able to exposit the Bible flawlessly and explain the gospel clearly, but to not apply its truths to our hearts. I have sat with many learned seminary professors, biblical scholars, and seasoned pastors who could expertly exegete the gospel of grace but who have wept tears of frustration and sadness because they were unable to apply the truth of the gospel to their hearts, unable to see that God loved them, and unable to receive the grace available to them. This is why applying the truth to our hearts is an essential part of the transformation process.

Although difficult, challenging our false beliefs will enrich our lives. Because it is helpful to have an objective sounding board, you may want to consider getting help from others, including friends, family, or a wise coach or counselor.

REFLECTION QUESTIONS

1. Identify a memory of an experience that you have had where the meaning you ascribed to that experience was inaccurate.
2. How did the inaccurate meaning you ascribed to your experience affect your view of self, your view of others, and your view of God?
3. Identify two or three false beliefs that you have had in the past or currently have about yourself, other people, or God (e.g., "I am a failure," "I'll never achieve anything in life," "I'm not lovable," "God is against me").

Using each of the false beliefs above, answer the following questions:
   a. Is the belief (always) *true*?
   b. What is the *evidence* for my belief?
   c. What *false assumptions* am I making?
4. With respect to the above false beliefs you have carried, how would your life change if you walked according to the truth?

Chapter 18
A PERSONAL PLAN FOR TRANSFORMATION

This chapter will guide us in creating our personal narratives to help integrate what we have learned about the genesis of our ruling passions and the pervasiveness of their impact on our lives and ministries today. In the next chapter I share my story of addressing my ruling passions, and the appendix has two more stories. You may find it helpful to read these stories before writing yours to see some examples of the form it may take. Knowing our stories will first equip us with a broader perspective and robust understanding to make sense of our stories and enable us to prayerfully make informed choices about areas of our lives that we desire to change, experience transformation, and require repentance. Then, we can be good stewards of our past and offer ourselves as a gift to others. But we must know every nook and cranny of our stories. In his book *Leading with a Limp*, Dan Allender writes,

> We can't offer our story to others, unless we are aware of the . . . context of our own story. Character is formed in

the midst of hearing and telling the full story. . . . If he plunges into his own story, then he will understand better, where he refuses to live with faith, hope, and love. He will better be able to name how he attempts to make truth serve his own idolatry rather than allowing the lies of his life to be exposed by the searing goodness of God. We lead others to God, only to the degree that we are aware of how much we flee him, how little we truly desire him, and yet how God is also the deepest, true, and sweetest desire of our hearts.[1]

As you embark on this endeavor, realize that you are not simply writing your story. Rather, as Allender writes, "*You are a story.* You are not merely the possessor . . . of a number of stories. You are a well-written, intentional story that is authored by the greatest writer of all time, and even before time and after time."[2] God truly is the Creator of your unique life and seeks to reveal his glory in and through your story.

On the Personal Worksheet below is a series of questions to help you find your ruling passions and understand them in the context of your story. This step-by-step approach is illustrated in figure 5.

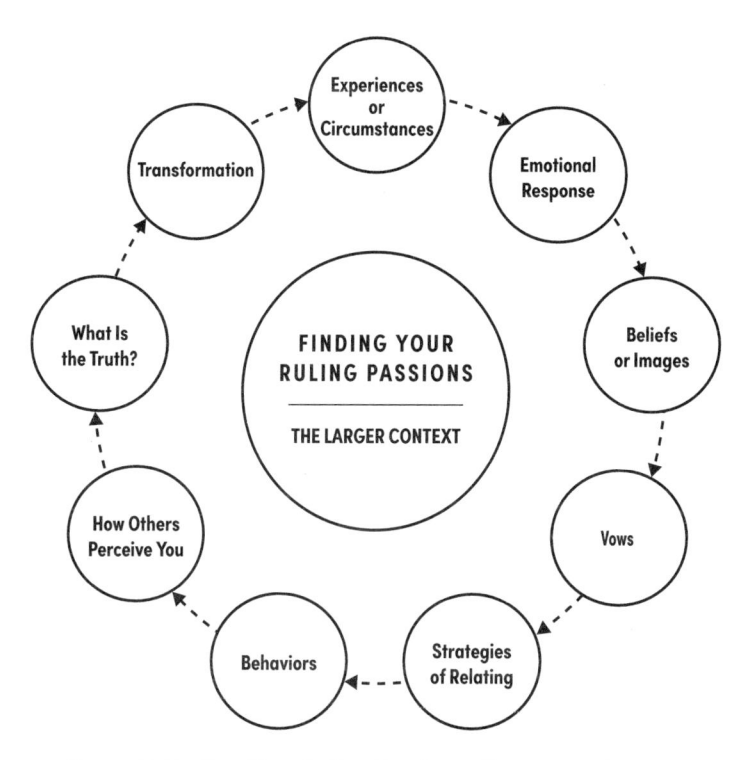

Figure 5: Finding Your Ruling Passions: The Larger Context

Although this illustration begins with the shaping "experiences and circumstances" that significantly influenced you and moves clockwise, you *may begin at any point* on this flow chart and work forward or backward. As you answer these questions, try to be as specific and detailed as possible. It is easy to brush over difficult facts and experiences, but it is in our pain that God draws near to us. We are wise to heed Dan Allender's advice:

> Most of us tell stories regarding the heartache of the past in a manner that allows us to tell the truth without being

transformed by it. We tell without telling. We allow details to be generalized and painful parts to be suppressed. And no one seems to notice or enter the forbidden terrain with a call to clarity or an invitation to grieve. The result is that our memories don't call us to God in the present. People seldom remember in a way that causes them to be desperate for God to be God.[3]

Thus, be brave and embrace the multiple complex facets of your story. Prayerfully engage with God and others so that you can begin to see your story through Christ's redemptive and grace-filled eyes.

Each of the steps will be illustrated by Bruce's story. Bruce is a seasoned church planter who has been in ministry for over forty years. He was the director of a church planter assessment center, oversaw a regional church planting network in a major denomination, helped plant more than twenty-five churches, taught practical theology at a seminary, and served as the pastor of four churches.

PERSONAL WORKSHEET
Finding Your Ruling Passions

Use the questions and illustration below as a step-by-step guide to help you find your ruling passions and create your personal narrative. If you have completed the preliminary exercises in chapter 5, you may use that information and develop it more fully.

1. What shaping *experiences or circumstances* were significant in my life?

2. What was my *emotional response* to those experiences?

3. What *beliefs* about my world or myself did I form or adopt because of my experiences?

4. What *vows* did I make because of my beliefs?

5. How do I relate to others as a result of my vows?

6. What *behaviors* do I engage in as I relate to other people to fulfill my vows?

7. How do *others perceive* me based on my behaviors and the way I relate to them? How do the ways others perceive and treat me *reinforce my beliefs* about my world or myself?

8. Are these *beliefs true* and biblical, or are they *false*? Why? If my beliefs are false, what is the truth? Am I looking at myself and my beliefs through a biblical lens? What would God say to me about the false beliefs I have about myself and others?

9. What does true transformation look like? Can I see my story—even my pain and suffering—through the lens of God's providential hand in my life? How could I be a good steward of my past and use it to glorify God and love others? How would my life change as I am transformed into the image of Christ? Be specific.

STEP 1: WHAT SHAPING EXPERIENCES OR CIRCUMSTANCES WERE SIGNIFICANT IN YOUR LIFE?

Begin by identifying specific circumstances, experiences, or a constellation of experiences in your life that had a profound positive or negative impact on you and shaped who you are today. "Circumstances" include many diverse aspects of your life including your family of origin, birth order, relationship with your parents and siblings, socioeconomic status, race, education, intelligence, disability, and significant experiences you had as a child, teen, or adult.[4]

Look for circumstances that gave rise to pain or pleasure in your life. Were you born into a relatively healthy family that cared well for you or were you neglected or criticized? Did you suffer trauma, painful losses, or emotional, physical, or sexual abuse? Or you may have had enjoyable or pleasurable experiences that caused you to make a vow. What were your family's values? What were the "commandments" in your family?[5] Were there "earthquake" events such as illnesses, untimely deaths, suicides, abandonments, or rejections? What messages were given by your parents or significant others that you internalized?[6]

Bruce's shaping experiences or circumstances

Bruce was the oldest son in a family of five siblings. A seminal experience in his life that caused him to develop his ruling passion was being abandoned by his father. Here is how he described this excruciating experience that affected him for the rest of his life:

> When I was eight years old, my father left my family without any explanation. I woke up one morning and my father was gone. I did not know other kids who had been abandoned by their father and this was a time when divorce was rare. As the only person in my class who came from

a divorced home, I was ridiculed and bullied. My mother was a "divorcée," and I felt the sting of that strange status. I felt odd, different, and defective. I cried myself to sleep every night. I was also angry and got into a lot of fights in school. I would fight anyone who picked on me—it did not matter their size—if they messed with me, I made them pay. I was the oldest boy in our home; a friend of my mother's told me that I was now the "man of the house." I took on the responsibilities of taking care of the house and yard. I prematurely took on a parental role, feeling responsible for my mother and my younger siblings.

As you can see in Bruce's story, his experience of his father leaving left deep scars, confusion, and emotional pain that he dealt with in the only way he knew how at the time. However, not all shaping experiences need to be based out of severe trauma or abandonment. Even a seemingly "small" event or memory can have a huge impact. Take the time to sit with your story and formative events and invite the Holy Spirit to guide your thinking as you process and explore your story.

STEP 2: WHAT EMOTIONAL RESPONSE DID YOU HAVE TO YOUR SHAPING EXPERIENCES OR CIRCUMSTANCES?

In this step, take the time to honestly explore the emotions you felt arising from the circumstances you described in step 1. List or describe how you responded emotionally to that event. Common emotions include pain, shame, loneliness, frustration, emptiness, anger, anxiety, numbness, or hardness, or a combination of emotions. Notice what you felt at the time of the event and what you are presently feeling as you reflect on your past experiences.

A PERSONAL PLAN FOR TRANSFORMATION

If you don't feel anything or are not feeling the emotions you expected, be patient. Some find it difficult to feel or express emotions. Allow yourself to spend some time in prayer and reflection, asking God to help you feel. Asking yourself, how someone else might feel had they had your experience can be helpful. You may find it helpful to review chapter 15 on processing emotions and intentionally walk through that process.

Bruce's emotional response

Bruce described his emotional response to his father's abandonment as "indescribable and intolerable deep hurt." Bruce cried himself to sleep every night. He was angry, both at his father and himself:

> What's wrong with me that my dad left me? In private I was hurt; in public I was angry and got into fights with the other kids. At one point I punched my third grade teacher in the face when she tried to break up a fight. I felt lonely, unloved, and deficient. These emotions were a common and pervasive feeling for a large part of my life.

As we will see in step 3, these experiences and his emotional response to them began to shape Bruce's beliefs about himself and his world.

STEP 3: WHAT BELIEFS AND IMAGES DID YOU DEVELOP?

In this step, try to identify the beliefs you have developed from the circumstances and emotional responses you have described above. These include beliefs developed about yourself, others, life, your world, and God. Beliefs about oneself can be positive or negative. At this point, we are not asking whether your beliefs are true; that is for another step. Here are some common negative beliefs:

- I'm not lovable.
- I'm all alone.
- I'm ugly.
- I'm doomed.
- I have no value.
- I have nothing to offer.
- Nothing really matters.
- I'm not confident.
- I never get it right.
- I am inferior.
- I don't have what it takes.
- I won't care anymore.
- I am stupid.
- No one cares about me.
- The world is dangerous.
- I can't trust others.
- I will be abandoned.
- I am helpless.

Here are some common positive beliefs:

- I am good.
- I am lovable.
- I have what it takes.
- I'm the best.
- I can handle this.
- It will go well with me.
- I can control myself.
- I have some control in life.

- I'm going to win.
- I'll do the best I can and that's all that is required.
- I don't have to be perfect.
- I am valued.[7]

In addition to beliefs, we can develop visual images in our own minds that summarize our beliefs in pictorial form. A close friend of mine had the image of himself always standing alone outside, looking through a window at a gathering of people who were laughing and having fun. This image was a metaphor for how he regarded himself as an outsider, always alone and separated from groups of people who were connected to each other. When we have beliefs and images about ourselves, they can shape a larger, inaccurate lens through which we interpret other experiences. These beliefs can set us up for developing behavioral strategies of relating that influence the way others see us and relate to us.

Bruce's beliefs and images

As a result of being abandoned by his father, Bruce developed a network of interdependent beliefs. He articulated them like this:

> I'm intrinsically flawed—there is something deeply wrong with me. Others are unreliable; I can't depend on anyone to love or stay with me. Therefore, I can only depend on myself. I must protect myself from the pain of rejection and abandonment; I'll be my own best friend.

Notice that although they are false, each of Bruce's beliefs are logically connected to each other. The belief that he had to protect himself from painful close relationships and from future abandonment became a dominant narrative in his life and ministry and a lens through which he interpreted the "data" of further experiences.

STEP 4: WHAT VOWS DID YOU MAKE AS A RESULT OF YOUR BELIEFS?

A vow is an expression of the heart, an internal commitment that articulates a decision about the way we will live our lives and how we will pursue what we are most passionate about. They express the *organizing principles* around which we base our lives and engage our world to satisfy our longings for, among other things, relationships, love, affirmation, acceptance, security, creativity, and impact on others and our world. Our vows can be made anytime during our lives at any age and can be articulated simply and concisely.

Articulate the vows you have made because of your beliefs. See whether you can explore some of the vows that you have made which are just below the surface of your awareness.

Bruce's vows

As a result of Bruce's beliefs that he had to protect himself from the pain he felt from his father's abandonment, he made several vows, each of which is interconnected:

> I will not be hurt again. I cannot trust anyone with my heart. I'll protect myself from the pain of rejection. I will never let anyone get too close to me or know me well. I will hide my flaws. I can only rely on myself.

These vows informed strategies he developed for relating with others.

STEP 5: HOW DO YOU RELATE TO OTHERS AS A RESULT OF YOUR VOWS?

Our vows inform our *strategies of relating*—how we will consistently relate to others to bring about the goals embedded in our vows.[8] The decision to engage in these relational strategies can be conscious and deliberate or unconsciously chosen. My brother had a core belief that people would reject him and so his strategy of relating involved saying and doing outrageously inappropriate things. He believed it was better to be in control of the rejection. Being rejected for himself was too painful.

Sometimes small interactions will give you clues about your strategies. A friend's ruling passion for control leaked out as he encouraged me to connect with his friend. He said, "Dave, I want you to call Ed and say, 'Hi Ed, my name is Dave Wiedis. I'm calling because Tom told me you would be interested in ServingLeaders Ministries.'" Now, think about this—Tom is a sophisticated, experienced businessman, telling me, another grown, experienced man, the precise words to say to the extent of telling me literally to say, "My name is Dave Wiedis." His ruling passion for control leaked out even in this most innocuous setting—as if I did not know my name or realize I needed to introduce myself using my name.

How would you describe your strategies for relating to others? Can you identify specific choices you have made? Here are some examples of strategies for relating with other people that can arise from our vows:

- I will be nice.
- I will act confrontational and aggressive.
- I will act as a peacemaker.
- I will be helpful.
- I will withdraw and be shy.

- I will make people laugh.
- I will act aloof and above it all.
- I will act as the intellectual.
- I will impress others.
- I will act coyly and seductively.
- I will be mysterious.
- I will be cold and distant.

Bruce's strategies of relating

Bruce's vows to not depend on or trust others, to avoid rejection, to hide his flaws, and to be self-reliant affected virtually every relationship with his family and church. He described his relational strategies particularly as they had a bearing on his marriage and pastoral ministry:

> As a young man in high school and college, I did not date for fear of getting hurt. After I got married, I hid my weaknesses and the parts of my personality that I found unacceptable from my wife because I feared she would lose respect for me. I simply kept the best parts of myself hidden and did not give my heart totally to her because I feared that if she really knew me, she would leave.
>
> As a pastor, I did not enter deeply into relationships. I kept most of my congregants at a safe distance and I stayed emotionally aloof from virtually everyone, even my elders. I simply did not allow others to see my heart or let anyone get close to me. With respect to ministry events and major projects, I remained self-reliant; I kept my ideas close to the vest, and I tended to micromanage the various ministries that we had.

STEP 6: WHAT BEHAVIORS DO YOU ENGAGE IN AS YOU RELATE TO OTHERS?

Our relational strategies manifest in objectively observable behaviors that can be seen, perceived, and described by others. For example, the person who relates to others as a peacemaker will engage in observable behaviors that are consistent with peacemaking. They may appear nonconfrontational, speak respectfully, and display sensitivity. The person who develops an outgoing, demonstrative strategy of relating may be gregarious and loud and demand attention consistent with that strategy.

Reflect on the behaviors that you engage in that stem from your strategies of relating to others. What would others observe you doing in specific situations? If you need help, ask a trusted friend or family member to provide feedback.

Bruce's behaviors

Bruce engaged in behaviors that were consistent with his vows of self-reliance and fear of abandonment. He said,

> As a pastor, I concentrated on acquiring the skills and competencies of ministry. These included public giftedness, preaching, teaching, and coaching. Relationships in ministry were secondary to me. I focused on tasks, on "getting things done for Jesus." I needed to get people "on the team," to focus on ministry activities, and if you observed me, you would see me preaching well, organizing events, encouraging others, coaching people in their spiritual walk and understanding Scripture and theology. However, I kept people at arm's length, and my ability to communicate my love for them was deeply compromised. People in my church did not feel I truly loved them, or that I was motivated primarily out of love for them. It's

hard to admit now, but they felt used by me rather than loved by me.

Concerning conflict, Bruce noted,

I engaged in conflict the same way I did in grade school, except in church my "weapons" were words and an aggressive attitude rather than my fists. If there was conflict, I ran toward it to win the argument before someone had the chance to reject or criticize me.

STEP 7: HOW DO OTHERS PERCEIVE AND TREAT YOU AS A RESULT OF YOUR BEHAVIORS?

Others will observe our behaviors and form opinions about us based on their perceptions. They will act in a way consistent with their perceptions of us. Gaining insight into how others perceive us is an invaluable resource. It allows us to see the impact we have on others and can play a critical role in how we see ourselves. Significantly, how others perceive and behave toward us can serve to *confirm* our own beliefs—even false beliefs—about ourselves.

For example, if I falsely believe that I am not lovable, I may make a vow never to allow anyone to get close to me. I'll adopt a strategy of relating to others to keep people away, perhaps by being unfriendly, aloof, or downright rude and mean. Others who perceive my mean behavior will likely stay away. Their behavior—staying away from me—then reinforces my false belief that I'm not lovable. As this cycle is repeated, it strengthens that false belief. When this cycle repeats, we can feel hopelessly trapped and convinced of the truth of our false belief without a conscious awareness of the role we have played in creating and perpetrating it.

How others perceived Bruce

In reflecting on how others perceived him, Bruce observed,

> My wife perceived me as withholding emotional closeness. She responded to this by staying distant from me. Because she was also independent, self-reliant, and tended to avoid conflict, our marriage was relatively free of conflict. However, the price we paid for this was a lack of true emotional intimacy that we both desired.

He further observed that their lack of emotional intimacy confirmed his false belief that "I am deeply flawed and cannot depend on anyone, even my wife, to love or stay with me."

Similarly, with respect to his church, Bruce observed,

> My congregation perceived me as being competent in the tasks of ministry, independent, and self-reliant. They also felt my emotional distance and my lack of relational care for them. Although I effectively enlisted people to help in ministry activities, over time people perceived me as staying relationally uninvolved and unloving. Because I also aggressively ran toward conflict, people avoided confronting me about problems they observed in the church or that I created by becoming withdrawn or being prone to unhelpfully engage in conflict. Most people in my church did not provide feedback to me that would have been valuable for me to hear and improve as a pastor. Some left my church.

When people left his church, it reinforced Bruce's (false) belief that he was defective and would be abandoned by those who really knew him. This cycle repeated itself over the years in other churches Bruce pastored and in other contexts. Bruce's pattern of behavior perpetuated a cycle of people leaving him; this confirmed his false beliefs about himself ("See, I am flawed, unlovable, defective") and others ("See, I can't trust others; they did abandon me").

Ironically, Bruce longed for love and acceptance but his ruling passion to be independent and not rely on others prevented him from getting what he longed for. Experiencing this cycle for many years in different churches, Bruce felt pervasive feelings of discouragement, self-doubt, and depression that resulted in a serious personal crisis for him and his ministry. Being able to fully understand his story and reflect on how his ruling passions caused him to behave in ways that were antithetical to loving others has helped him engage in repentance and experience transformation.

STEP 8: ARE YOUR BELIEFS TRUE?

As we saw in chapter 17, a fundamental question we must ask ourselves is whether our beliefs are true or false using both Scripture and reality as our standard. The belief that "I'm not lovable" can be tested by what the Word of God says about God's love for people. The lies we believe can be replaced and transformed by the biblical truth that God's love for me is unconditional and inexhaustible. As you consider whether your beliefs are true, recall that Satan is the father of lies; his lies can be hard to uncover and difficult to shake.

Take the beliefs that you identified in step 3 and reflect on whether they are true in light of the truths of Scripture. If they are false, replace them with the truth. As explained in chapter 17, to find and walk in the truth, you may find it helpful to answer the following questions:

- Is the belief (always) *true*?
- What is the *evidence* for my belief?
- What *false assumptions* am I making?

Were Bruce's beliefs true?

One of the fundamental flaws in Bruce's thinking was that as a young boy, he adopted the false belief that he was intrinsically flawed and defective. As we have seen, this arose from the meaning he derived from his experience of being abandoned by his father. But does his belief that he is defective make it so, or is it based on erroneous reasoning, false assumptions, and wrong conclusions? How does a father's independent choice to abandon his family make Bruce defective? This is the thinking of a child, not a rational adult. It is a lie and is not in line with God's Word; it violates it. It was crucial for Bruce to understand that his ruling passion to be self-reliant and independent and his relational style created the environment for people to abandon him, and this confirmed his false belief that he was intrinsically flawed.

With respect to Bruce's false beliefs, here are some truths that he came to realize. Bruce's father divorced his mother and abandoned his family due to a host of reasons that had nothing to do with Bruce's intrinsic character or behavior. His father had his own painful experiences growing up in a dysfunctional family and learned to cope with painful obstacles and relationships by avoiding them. Bruce's father had the responsibility to make godly, healthy choices when he faced the issues in his life that ultimately caused him to leave his family. Bruce's father sinned against him and his family by abandoning them. God loves Bruce and has been actively working in his life from the time he was born through the present.

STEP 9: WHAT DOES TRANSFORMATION LOOK LIKE?

As we integrate all of the circumstances and events that caused us to develop our specific ruling passions, as we understand the truth that God uses suffering to mature us, as we see through the lens of God's sovereign reign and providential control in every detail of our lives, and as we believe that "all things work together for good" (Romans 8:28), the perspective, narrative, and trajectory of our lives will dramatically change. Our hearts' dispositions will be toward the supremacy of Christ ruling in our lives. We will be able to use our memories of the past to glorify God and love others. And we will be more likely to experience the sanctification and transformation to which Paul referred in Romans 12:2.

Take some time to prayerfully write out a statement that reflects what true transformation looks like in your life.

Bruce's transformation

In this final step, Bruce was able to experience the process of transformation by replacing his false beliefs with the truth of God's unconditional love. Here is how he completed this exercise.

> As I reflect on my ruling passions, I can now see that in God's sovereignty, he placed me in my particular family for a specific purpose. When my father abandoned us, God was there with me the entire time, hurting along with me. It makes perfect sense that as a young child, without the benefit of maturity, being able to think more rationally, and the wisdom of experience, I saw myself as defective and blamed myself for my father's leaving us. It also makes sense that I experienced deep, excruciating

A PERSONAL PLAN FOR TRANSFORMATION

pain that I did not have the capacity to handle in a mature way. I can see that I reacted to my pain by vowing to never trust others and to never allow others to get close to me, lest they find my flaws. I was tender on the inside but hardened on the outside. This led me to hide myself from my wife. As a pastor, I kept my congregants and elders at a safe distance, focusing on the tasks of ministry and evangelism within my areas of competence.

Now, as I have a clearer perspective of my longings and motives, I can see that although my quest to avoid pain was legitimate, the way I achieved it was sinful and hurtful. In the name of "self-protection," I failed to love and shepherd those in my congregation who needed me to be available to them.

I can see how God is redemptive and that nothing goes to waste. He is redeeming my sins, pain, and failures in a new season of my life. As I move forward in my capacities as a husband, pastor, and coach, I have softened inside and have opened my heart to my wife and others. I am no longer motivated by protecting myself from further pain and fear of abandonment; I truly care for people, and I desire to use my past painful experiences to glorify God and serve others with the wisdom that I have gained.

Doing this kind of story work is intensely personal; there is no right or wrong way to do it. The depth to which you complete these questions is up to you and can vary depending on your needs. It certainly takes a lot of honest reflection, prayerful meditation, and hard work. You may find it more helpful to do this in smaller steps, or with the help of a counselor or coach. I share my story in the next chapter and have provided other narratives in the appendix on page 225.

Chapter 19
PUTTING IT ALL TOGETHER
My Story

This book was born out of a seminar entitled "Your Ruling Passions: How the Idols of Your Heart Can Sabotage Your Life, Ministry, and Marriage." One of the sessions that people find most helpful is when I share my journey with my ruling passions. I do this to practically help people identify our ruling passions, illustrate how our ruling passions permeate virtually every aspect of our lives, demonstrate the process of repentance, and provide an example of a redemptive narrative. I share my story of failures and weakness here with the hope that you will find it helpful, keeping in mind that God's "power is made perfect in weakness" (2 Corinthians 12:9). As I share my story, I strongly believe that our defeats should not be hidden away; it is only when they are shared openly that valuable lessons can be learned for the future.

BACKGROUND FOR MY RULING PASSION
The predominant ruling passion I have struggled with throughout my entire life is to not be lonely. I often feel an

existential emptiness combined with a deep-seated insecurity about myself, feelings of inadequacy, and a sense that I do not have much to offer. Growing up, I was always conscious of having deep longings for closeness, intimacy, and friendship. I also longed to be regarded as "special" in someone else's eyes.

Where did these feelings come from? The answer is far more complex than can be explained here, and I don't know all the factors that worked together to produce these feelings. However, I believe it is partly a combination of my innate personality disposition and the environment in which I grew up.

I grew up in a Jewish family; I did not hear the gospel until well into my teen years. I was the middle child with an older brother and a younger sister. My parents were loving, kind, and involved in my life. They always showed an interest in my pursuits, attended my sports events, and provided for my needs. Although my father was gentle, caring, and empathetic, he could also be self-absorbed. He tended to turn our conversations back to him, his past, and his needs. Sometimes it felt like he was talking *at* me rather than *with* me. As a young boy I did not know this cognitively and did not have the capacity to explain this, but I sensed it, and it likely made me feel emotionally isolated. As I grew older and could discuss this with him, he was honest and admitted this tendency; he was open to feedback and always sought to improve himself.

My mother was a stereotypical Jewish mother and got a lot of joy out of our relationship. She admired me and let me know it. She was so proud when she could introduce me as "My son, the lawyer!" She suffered from chronic anxiety and depression but tried to hide it. I could see how suffering affected her; I suspect this likely contributed to my feelings of insecurity and loneliness.

My parents were not good disciplinarians. In response to his own father's harshness, my father went to the other extreme of being too lenient and soft on us. My older brother (who we all jokingly referred to as having been born with sideburns) was out of control. At times he was my hero who protected me from bullies, and at other times he was my antagonist. He could be mean, unpredictable, and was physically abusive. The fact that he was six feet tall and about 225 pounds by the time he was fourteen only added to his imposing figure and to my anxiety.

My own disposition is an essential factor. I am an empathic soul and my parents taught me to pay attention to and express my feelings. I also experienced a lot of anxiety. I frequently had stomachaches from worrying about many imagined circumstances. Early in life, I experienced a lot of separation anxiety from my parents. Going away for two weeks to a sleepaway camp was a nightmare of feeling homesick.

With this background, I found being in relationships was a solace to me. When I hit adolescence and entered relationships with girls who were interested in me, I began to feel more alive and complete. Being seen, recognized, and admired felt great. I had several relationships that stemmed from and fostered emotional immaturity without fully understanding how these relationships impacted my heart. Because of early exposure to relational intimacy and sexual behavior, these early experiences reinforced the idea that to feel whole and significant, I had to be with someone who gave me the attention I desired. These relationships covered over my deep insecurities and my internal sense of not being whole. I developed an unhealthy dependence on relationships to give me a sense of self-worth, and I unconsciously developed a commitment to not be alone. The juxtaposition of feeling so alive when I was with someone and empty when I was not reinforced my longing to be known, admired, and loved. Given this background, my ultimate commitments or ruling passions could be articulated like this: I will not be lonely. I will organize my world in a way that makes me feel whole by being loved by another and seen as special and significant in her eyes.

RELATIONAL STRATEGIES TO FULFILL MY VOW

How did this play out? What relational strategies did I develop? I attached myself to someone else to feel significant. And so, as many teenagers do, I had several relationships that cemented my false beliefs that life was about finding that special someone to love me and make me feel whole. I really did not understand how deeply these beliefs took hold until I experienced heartbreak when I had my first breakup. I had no healthy categories with which to think about this. No one helped me understand that the beliefs I had developed about my lack of worth, significance, and value were false. At that time, I did not even consider the possibility that my thinking was wrong. *Ruling passions have a major impact on our relationship patterns and choices.*

MY RULING PASSION PERMEATED EVERY ASPECT OF MY LIFE

At the age of sixteen, I had a dramatic conversion experience and came to faith in Christ. This was powerful; for the first time, I experienced a deep love from God and felt more alive and significant than ever before. The reality of God's presence and involvement in my life became evident to me and others. I voraciously read Scripture, attended church (much to the chagrin of my Jewish family), and fed the spiritual hunger that had been awakened in me. I had good friends who invested in my spiritual growth, and I quickly wanted to share my faith with others. However, as real as my faith and this experience were, I was not instantly whole or healed from all my struggles. I remained unaware of my deeply held false beliefs that my value was rooted in being loved in the context of a romantic relationship. My exuberance in my newfound faith covered the profound emptiness inside. Many Christians labor under a major misconception that "getting saved" heals us from all our underlying emotionally unhealthy issues. It does not. As Peter Scazzero has emphasized, "It is not possible to be spiritually mature while remaining emotionally immature."[1] Much deeper, intentional work is needed. *Ruling passions are not automatically healed when one comes into a relationship with God.*

MY RULING PASSION IMPACTED MY RELATIONSHIP CHOICES

At the age of eighteen, I fell in love with a woman in our church and married her two years later. My subjective experience was that I genuinely loved my wife and that God had guided me to marry her. Objectively, I had not matured sufficiently or experienced enough differentiation from my parents to have a healthy marriage. I was simply unaware that a primary motivation for marriage was my fear of being lonely. If you had challenged me by suggesting that I was being driven by my fear of loneliness, I might have recognized something vaguely true about that idea, but I would have instantly denied it and given you some spiritual justification for getting married. I simply could not have admitted that I had "deep needs" for someone else or even a fear of being alone; it was too threatening and shameful for me to acknowledge or enter the pain of my own internal loneliness.

After I got married, I felt content and did not wrestle with loneliness. I began teaching high school and played an active role in our church. I chalked up my lack of loneliness to my spiritual development rather than the fact that I had my "fix" in my wife. After four and a half years of marriage, I was blindsided when she left me. I felt completely disoriented and alone. Although I was the "innocent" party, I failed to see the negative ways my emotional neediness, self-centeredness, and immaturity had impacted my wife. And because I had minimized my "loneliness issue," she felt a lot of pressure from me to come through for me in ways that were unhealthy and unsatisfying to her.

At the same time she left me, a family member died, and I was diagnosed with bilateral hip dysplasia. My attempts to drown my pain and find some semblance of identity in martial arts were thwarted. I experienced more profound pain than I had ever known; I went into a deep depression, and my self-worth spiraled downward into a sense of worthlessness. I struggled to function through this depression. One vivid memory of that time comes to mind. It felt like I was walking in quicksand as I went to my classroom wondering how I could compose myself enough to teach; the only thing I could focus on was putting one foot in front of the other.

What was happening? Internally, my world, my identity, and all I was about were falling apart. Disintegrating. Job's words were mine: "For the thing that I fear comes upon me, and what I dread befalls me" (Job 3:25). Indeed, what I most feared—being alone—came to pass. Looking back, I can see that God, in his grace, sometimes allows us to experience the things we fear and find most painful in order to address deep issues in our hearts and set us free from our sinful ruling passions. *Ruling passions can lie dormant and unseen until they become manifest through painful circumstances.*

MY RULING PASSIONS IMPACTED MY CAREER CHOICES

After my divorce, I decided to leave my job as a high school teacher. As I pondered a new career path, I found myself considering two different careers: becoming an attorney or an actor. On the surface, my motivations may have seemed good. As an actor, I could practice an art form and craft that could be challenging, beautiful, and fulfilling. As an attorney, I could serve others, pursue truth, and achieve justice for those in need. As I reflect today on my motivations, my ruling passion to not be lonely was the significant factor as I contemplated these decisions.

Becoming an actor would mean that my time would be spent in the intense schedule of rehearsals and performances and I could enjoy camaraderie with other actors. Time alone would be minimized. More importantly, I was driven by an inaccurate perception that if I became well-known, I would be more desirable, admired, more attractive to others, and less lonely. These desires for admiration, respect, and even adoration were additional motivations of which I was unaware.

Becoming an attorney was also, in part, driven by motivations like those for becoming an actor. Attorneys are often valued and seen as intelligent, esteemed, and respected. Attorneys also have very demanding schedules and spend huge amounts of time absorbed in the law practice. I ultimately decided to move away from my hometown, attended law school, and sought to gain respect and affirmation in the legal profession. *Ruling passions play an important role in vocational decisions.*

MY RULING PASSIONS IMPACTED MY LIFE AS A SINGLE MAN

What did the single life look like for me, given my ruling passion to not be lonely and my need to feel significant? Over the next ten years, I went through a series of romantic relationships, temporarily assuaging the empty loneliness I felt so deeply. If I had been more mature and understood the powerful impact of my ruling passions, I would have been open to the following questions: What is ruling my heart? What am I pursuing with the most passion? What is my motive for pursuing and staying in relationships, especially when I knew they were not healthy or that they would not end up in marriage? And to be more courageous and honest, I would have asked myself to reflect on the impact my ruling passions had on others. What does my girlfriend feel from me? Does she feel "used" by me? Does she feel the pressure to come through for me and satisfy me to get me out of my loneliness? Outwardly, I looked like a normal, nice professional pursuing a romantic relationship. Internally, although it sounds (and is) crass, that time in my life was a painful pursuit of relationships to ultimately satisfy *my* needs. During that time, I went through a series of romantic relationships, each of which ended painfully. We were not designed to attach and detach in intimate relationships. *Ruling passions play an important role in romantic pursuits.*

MY JOURNEY TOWARD CHANGE AND REPENTANCE

After several years, and by the grace of God, I began to realize some ugly truths about my relational style as I explored the following question: If my underlying motivation and ultimate commitment was to feel whole and avoid loneliness by entering a relationship with a woman, was I loving her or using her? I started to realize and admit that I did not love her for *who* she was, but I loved *what* she offered me—a relief from loneliness and the ability to feel significant. I began to understand that she served a *function* for me. And I began to see that I could, and did, manipulate my girlfriend in subtle ways to get me out of my loneliness. *The degree to which we are not aware of our motivations is the degree to which we can be dangerous to others.* We hurt others when we use them for our own means and purposes. Outwardly, I was not as crass as this sounds. However, on the inside, deep in my heart, I was using, not loving. If this sounds ugly and selfish, it is. If it sounds as if acting out of our ruling passions can hurt others with whom we are in a relationship, it can.

As God gave me insight into the motivations of my heart, I also started to cultivate more awareness of my impact on those around me. My ruling passions did not just affect my most intimate relationships; they impacted my friends, family, colleagues, and acquaintances. Thankfully, close, dear friends who loved me well cared enough about me to lovingly tell me how I impacted them: they felt subtle pressure to come through for me or to function for me, and they felt subtly manipulated by me. As I became aware of my motivations and the impact I had on others, I started to first admit and face my ruling passions. I started to experience significant repentance by making different choices in how I interacted with and related to others.

A watershed moment in my life came when I was face-to-face with significant temptation. After graduating from law school, I treated myself to a trip to Europe—by myself. Spiritually I had been drifting from God over the previous few years, but I was just beginning to trust him again. As I traveled from Switzerland to Brugge, Belgium, I entered a private train compartment and sat down, staring at three beautiful women, all from the US. We made our introductions and bantered for a while. I could see they were fun and wanted to have a good time. "Where are you going?" they asked me. "Brugge. Where are you going?" I asked. "Amsterdam!! Why don't you come with us?" they enthused. I thought to myself, *Hmm. Brugge, by myself . . . or Amsterdam. I have heard that Amsterdam is a wild city. Brugge, alone. Amsterdam—with three beautiful women.* Given my ruling passions, the pull toward Amsterdam was strong. I wavered in my mind. I knew I did not even have a hotel reservation in Brugge and would arrive alone at night. I thought about how much fun it would be to go with these women. And I would not be alone.

But I also knew that trying to satisfy my feelings of emptiness in this way would ultimately leave me hurting and lonelier, and I would not honor God and my relationship with him. It would also dishonor and misuse these women in ways that God never intended. I would once again be using others to "function" for me to suit my purposes. Using sex to get relief from loneliness can be a dangerous and addictive combination. The meaning of sex can become very twisted, and using others for one's own gratification is a particularly insidious trap. As I thought my options through and wrestled with my longings not to be lonely, I asked God to help me make wise choices. By his grace, I determined to obey God at that moment and not give in to the power of my ruling passions.

What do you think it felt like as I stepped off the train that night in Brugge onto that station platform, alone and in the dark? It would be nice to say that my decision to obey God felt amazing and satisfying. No! It felt like death. I felt empty, anxious, and alone. For a while. And then, as I prayed and sought God, asking him to fill me, to derive my significance from his love, to allow me to know him and do the right thing, I started to feel better, more whole and less incomplete. And as God often (but not always) does, he came through for me in ways I did not expect. He showed himself to be faithful to me. I realized that nothing is more deeply satisfying than living out of a heart of love for God, choosing to obey him, and living according to his ways. When God enjoins us to keep his commandments that "it may go well with you," he is serious, and it is true.

That watershed moment on the train, choosing Brugge over Amsterdam, became a metaphor for gradual change and repentance through a deepening awareness of the impact of sinful ruling passions and a continual dependence on God in my weakness.

HOW GOD CHANGED ME

You may be wondering whether, since that experience in Brugge, I have experienced the transformation described in this book, and if so, what does that look like? What has it meant in my life? Does change mean I no longer get lonely, that I don't long for affirmation or try to derive significance from being seen as special? I'd love to tell you that I prayed and—*poof*—they disappeared, or that the presence of God is so tangible that I bask in his glow every day. The good news is that I am cultivating an ever-increasing awareness of the motivations of my heart and my impact on others; I am slowly changing. The bad news is that ruling passions are deep-seated and don't just vanish by force of reason, awareness, or even prayer. So how do I handle the strong competing desires between living out of my sinful ruling passions or the supremacy of Christ? The change I have experienced has taken place over time and is multifaceted.

First, my relationship with God is the most powerful influence on my heart. By God's grace, he pursues and loves me enough to not allow me to stay the same. As he convicts me of impure motives, I acknowledge and confess them. Instead of living in denial, I admit and recognize my tendency to use others. I regularly process my pain and longings, as outlined in chapter 15, by bringing them directly to God. I allow my weaknesses to drive me to Christ.

Second, God has given me the grace to do hard things by honestly facing my fears that are centered on my ruling passions. An unexpected job opportunity illustrates this. Years ago, I received a job offer that was completely outside of my expertise and experience with a ministry that I had admired for many years and had financially supported. I loved their mission to defend religious liberty, knew that it was run with integrity, and the role I would play was highly relational. However, taking the job meant taking a 50 percent pay cut, and required me to regularly travel across the country away from my family for extended periods at a time when my children were in elementary school. I loved practicing law, but this new job seemed like the perfect fit for me, and the offer came so unexpected that I felt I needed to pay attention. I entered an extended season of prayerful discernment with Miho and friends and had to squarely face my ruling passion to not be lonely. I also had to address losing the affirmation I received by leaving a "prestigious" position as a partner in my own law firm for what would be seen as a "less important" position.

As it became more apparent that God was leading me to accept the position, I balked inside. My ruling passion, having been dormant, began to create fear in my heart. I reasoned that I should not accept the position because "my children were young and needed me at home during their formative years. *They* will be lonely without me." As I reflected on my motives, I saw that I was engaging in both projection and rationalization. After all, whose needs was I really addressing—mine or theirs? Who was going to be lonely—me or them? I was engaging in rationalization by coming up with ostensibly plausible, even "godly," reasons to decline the offer and stay in my law firm. I reasoned that by staying home, I would be a responsible father, involved in the day-to-day details of my children's lives. Wouldn't God want that?

In prayer, I asked God to reveal my true motivations and follow his call. It was as if God asked me, "Who can better provide for your children's needs while you are away—you or me? Do you think that I can take care of your children and perform my work in their hearts while you are away on business trips? What would it look like to trust me in this? What is more important—being seen as having a prestigious position as a trial attorney in your firm, or following my calling to serve others in a less visible, supportive role?" The choice became clear. Trusting God's providential leading to care for me, my future career, and my children's needs was a much better option than being ruled by my fears and ruling passion.

The new position was very challenging, and there were many times I had to face my loneliness and anxieties. I grew as a result, and God developed character and resilience in me and my family. Facing my fears reinforced my desire not to allow my ruling passion to rule me. I could not have known at that time that by accepting that new position, God gave me the experiences, insights, and provisions that were necessary to create ServingLeaders Ministries seven years later. Most importantly, he gave me the resolve to continually seek the supremacy of Christ's rule in my life.

Third, my marriage is a fertile ground for continual change. Four years after my trip to Brugge, I married Miho. We have shared our respective ruling passions with each other, know ourselves and each other well, and are not blindsided by our ruling passions. When she feels pressured by me or senses I am motivated by my ruling passion, she has appropriate and healthy boundaries; she is strong enough to lovingly resist and challenge me. Many spouses don't have the strength to resist and try to satisfy areas in their spouse's lives that only God can satisfy. This can develop into an unhealthy codependency and harm the relationship. We both have permission to address these areas in each other's lives; her loving feedback has been the catalyst for real change.

Fourth, I have greatly benefited from seeking professional individual and marital counseling to explore the origins of my ruling passions and develop further strategies for dealing with them. Counseling can help us have a broader perspective on areas of our lives that are puzzling and mysterious, bring to light the lies we believe, and work through difficult issues that seem to be lifelong afflictions. Counseling can have a profound impact on our relationship with God, on the sanctification process, and on our relationships with others.

Finally, I have been blessed with good friends and a healthy church community who don't abandon me when I stumble, but rather stay close and loving. When people are honest and authentic, we experience unconditional love in a tangible way. Being in a healthy, loving community is essential for our growth and sanctification. And it was *in community* where Peter interacted with the Gentile Christians, where Paul confronted Peter, where he helped him repent of his ruling passion, and ultimately where their relationship healed (Galatians 2:11–17; 2 Peter 3:14–16).

Chapter 20
SO MUCH TO LOSE, EVERYTHING TO GAIN

The message in this book about our ruling passions is not theoretical to me. As an attorney and counselor, I have seen many on a seemingly harmless trajectory, but their lives and ministries ended badly. There is no greater calling than to wholeheartedly respond to God's invitation to a deeper relationship with him and be changed. There is no greater joy than seeing the fruit of a surrendered and passionate life, loving and leading others in a way that will have an eternal kingdom ripple effect. But to do this well, we must look both upward and inward, or as Paul warned Timothy, we must "keep a close watch on [ourselves] and on the teaching" (1 Timothy 4:16).

As a loving mentor, Paul knew of risks to Timothy, and I know of risks to all of us who desire our ruling passion to be Jesus. No one is immune from self-sabotage. Many forces compete for our heart's affection; many passions want to rule us. To redeem our passions, we must be surrendered to the lordship of Christ and guided by the Holy Spirit. We must live as Jesus lived. We may pursue many passions, but Jesus must be our main passion. We must also grow awareness of our specific propensities to engage in idolatry by making good things into ultimate things. This was precisely the blind spot that Paul confronted in Peter, and I hope this book is an echo of Paul's voice, reminding us of how dangerous these hidden idols can be.

You might be tempted to lean on your theological training, knowledge of Scripture, or track record so far to safeguard your life from idolatry that underlies moral failure or weakened faith. Many great leaders have foolishly relied on the same. Let me gently remind you that the apostle Peter had the most robust resume and powerful spiritual experiences than any believer could have. Peter did not wake up one morning and decide to intentionally hurt his Gentile flock. But the seeds of self-sabotage had already been sown decades before and lay dormant in the soil of his heart. Peter may have believed that he was insulated from his ruling passions based on *his* training, knowledge, and experiences with Jesus, which far exceeded our experiences. Yet it wasn't enough. It wasn't enough to have been personally called by Jesus and have left everything to follow and live with him. It wasn't enough to have been given special revelation so he could identify Jesus as the Messiah. Nor was it enough to be one of the three most eminent apostles, to bravely preach and lead thousands to salvation, to heal people, or even to raise a woman from the dead (Acts 9:34, 40). Nor was it enough to receive a vision directly from God (Acts 10:9–11). None of these immunized Peter from his ruling passion that undermined his ministry and hurt his friends and church family.

The only way for you to redeem your passions is to be curious, honest, humble, and open about the desires of your heart with yourself, your close community, and Jesus, with complete surrender and confidence in the power and passion of Jesus. It was Jesus who perfectly surrendered himself to the Father's will, desiring what the Father desires in perfect and complete alignment. It was Jesus whose ruling passion for his Father's will and glory, for the joy set before him, endured the cross to bring you, with your passions and desires, back to life in him for his glory! When we understand that our life in Christ is an utterly undeserved gift and that the blessings he gives us in this life must always be traced back to the source, then our one true desire will be him. And when Christ is our ruling passion, the reward is immeasurable and indescribable and will reverberate through eternity. We have everything to gain.

Appendix
STORIES OF RULING PASSIONS

As you consider your ruling passions and their impact on your life, you may find it helpful to read accounts of others who have explored their ruling passions. Included below are some examples of personal narratives. There are many ways to write your story. You can provide detailed or short answers to the questions from the Personal Worksheet in chapter 18, which are reprinted below. You may choose to write your narrative in the third person or first person. I encourage you to be creative and write your story in a way that will best help you understand your story, how your ruling passions have impacted your life, and the best course to repentance.

1. What shaping *experiences or circumstances* were significant in my life?
2. What was my *emotional response* to those experiences?
3. What *beliefs* about my world or myself did I form or adopt because of my experiences?
4. What *vows* did I make because of my beliefs?

5. How do I relate to others as a result of my vows?
6. What *behaviors* do I engage in as I relate to other people to fulfill my vows?
7. How do *others perceive* me based on my behaviors and the way I relate to them? How do the ways others perceive and treat me *reinforce my beliefs* about my world or myself?
8. Are these *beliefs true* and biblical, or are they *false*? Why? If my beliefs are false, what is the truth? Am I looking at myself and my beliefs through a biblical lens? What would God say to me about the false beliefs I have about myself and others?
9. What does true transformation look like? Can I see my story—even my pain and suffering—through the lens of God's providential hand in my life? How could I be a good steward of my past and use it to glorify God and love others? How would my life change as I am transformed into the image of Christ? Be specific.

SHARON'S STORY

Sharon serves as a missionary. She sought counseling because she felt depressed and inadequate in her ministry. She tended to stuff her feelings until she blew up in anger, and she had a very negative view of herself in virtually every area of life. She engaged in constant negative self-talk filled with condemnation for herself as a wife, mother, friend, and missionary on the field. She reported that she felt numb for long periods of time. However, at unexpected times, she would be overcome by her emotions, burst into tears, and then cry uncontrollably for hours. She was upset and angry with her coworkers, feeling judged and ignored by them.

Step 1: Sharon's shaping experiences and circumstances

Sharon's parents divorced when she was four years old. She lived with her mother who was critical of her and always expressed disappointment with her. Nothing Sharon did was ever good enough for her mother; she felt unloved by her father who was uninvolved and distant. He repeatedly broke his promises to spend time with her and sometimes he would not contact her for months. She remembers longing to be with him. A significant painful childhood memory was that of anticipating her father visiting her after a long absence. He had promised to pick her up from her home and take her out, but then simply failed to show up. When he was present, he was distracted, paid little attention to her needs, and gave her the distinct impression that he did not want her around.

Step 2: Sharon's emotional responses

As a result of feeling criticized by her mother and unwanted by her father, Sharon felt many emotions that she described as *excruciating pain*. She felt *disappointed*, deeply *sad*, desperately *lonely*, and *unloved*. These emotions were a common and pervasive feeling for a large part of growing up and, as we will see in step 3, they began to shape her beliefs about herself and her world.

Step 3: Sharon's beliefs and images

As a result of her negative experiences, Sharon developed the following beliefs: "I don't matter," "I'm insignificant," "I don't do anything right," "I'm not preferred," "I'm not desirable," "I have no value." Notice that each of these beliefs is connected to a general feeling that she is inferior and "no good." She also described a poignant image of herself sitting at the end of her family's table while everyone else was gathered at the other end. They were happy, desired, and included, but she was not. This became a dominant theme and narrative in her life through which she interpreted the "data" of further experiences.

Step 4: Sharon's vows

As a result of Sharon's beliefs that she was not desired and had no value, she made several vows, each of which is interconnected: "I will not be hurt again," "I'll protect myself from my friends who can hurt me," "I will never let anyone get close to me," "When I sense I will be hurt, I will break off my relationships first." Significantly, as we probed more deeply, Sharon was also able to identify deeper vows regarding how she would deal with her own painful emotions: "I will kill my desire, and I will disconnect from my own longings because it's too painful to feel them." Her decision as a young girl to cope with her pain by numbing and disconnecting from her emotions makes sense and gives us insight into why she can turn her emotions off, seemingly at will.

Step 5: Sharon's strategies of relating

As a result of her vows to protect herself from relational pain, Sharon developed several relational strategies. She hid herself both emotionally and physically. She hid her true feelings about issues and remained quiet in business and social settings. If she was asked her opinion on doctrinal, political, or social issues, she hid it. On the mission field, she would operate independently, would stay "behind the scenes," and would be quite productive. Also, she was determined to appear competent, to be self-sufficient, and to not come across as being "needy."

Step 6: Sharon's behaviors

Sharon engaged in behaviors consistent with her strategies for hiding her feelings. Others observed her as alone, quiet, confident, staying in the background, and never asking for help. She acknowledged that she hid her femininity by overeating and gaining weight. When coworkers asked her to go out to lunch, she would always politely refuse. If anyone asked whether she needed help on projects, she politely declined.

Step 7: How others perceived Sharon

Others perceived Sharon as being quiet, self-sufficient, independent, and confident. Her coworkers would say, "She has it all together and wants to be left alone," and so they did. They stopped inviting her to go out for lunch or to engage in other social activities. This confirmed her (false) belief about herself (which originated from the way her father treated her) that she was undesirable and unlovable. Because her coworkers also perceived her as being competent and not needing help, they never offered to help her or to come alongside her as she engaged in projects. Nor did they seek her opinions because she tended to hide her opinions and feelings. Ironically (and sadly), others' perceptions of and their behaviors toward Sharon confirmed her false beliefs that she didn't matter, was insignificant, could not do anything right, was not preferred, was not desirable, and had no value! The more others left her alone, the more she felt isolated and alone. Her strategies of relating to her coworkers helped perpetuate the cycle of their behaviors that confirmed her false beliefs about herself. This further exacerbated her deep longing to be desired, loved, and sought after.

Step 8: The truth about Sharon

Sharon's subjective perceptions that she "could not do anything right" were belied by the objective performance reviews by her superiors and the respect she had from her coworkers on the field. Her false belief that she was "not desirable" resulted from her misinterpretation and the inaccurate meaning she ascribed to her coworkers not inviting her to be with them. They were honestly motivated by their belief that she preferred to be alone; not inviting her was an act of respect. She interpreted their behavior as confirming her belief that she was not desirable.

The gospel has much to say to a person who believes she does not matter, is insignificant, and has no value. Scripture reveals that humans made in his image have inestimable value; Jesus's sacrificial act of atonement for our sins establishes that we are significant and matter. Sharon's major challenge was to revise her story through the lens of God's love for her and to experience the emotional healing that takes place in working through her story in an environment where she experiences empathy, compassion, and acceptance.

Step 9: Transformation

Seeing herself through the loving, grace-filled eyes of Christ, Sharon was able to revise her story and experience the emotional healing that takes place in working through her story in an environment where she experienced empathy, compassion, and acceptance. She has repented of her strategy to protect herself from pain, and rather than withdrawing and hiding from others, she now offers herself as a gift to serve and love them. She sees herself as valuable, gaining significance from Christ's love, and has effectively served for many years.

LAURA'S STORY

Laura is a ministry leader who attended the Ruling Passions seminar and crafted the following narrative using the Personal Worksheet: Finding Your Ruling Passions:

My shaping circumstances and experiences

My parents are amazing people and yet still have wounding from their own stories that leaked out and impacted me during my formative years. When I was a child, my father was perfectionistic toward himself and tended to view the world in black and white. He deeply valued restraint and was vigilant about doing the right thing, being kind, and not inconveniencing people. As I grew up, I quickly picked up on this in my dad. My mom was emotionally fragile and wanted everyone to be happy. I sensed from a young age that there wasn't much room to express my emotions to her (particularly negative emotions), and she was most at peace when everyone around her was peaceful or seemed peaceful. She interpreted negative emotions from others personally, felt wounded by them, and was fearful of conflict. Early on I internalized the belief that conflict was scary and threatened relational closeness and that keeping people happy was the best way for things to feel peaceful. When I was thirteen, my older sister emotionally withdrew from our family, and her behaviors and attitude created significant relational upheaval in our family. My parents were distraught. As all of this was happening, I felt invisible because the focus was on my sister and the ways my parents were hurting over her choices. It hurt me deeply when I felt ignored or in the background, but I didn't know how to express how I felt, so I just started to work hard to *earn* attention, favor, and love. I believed that the only way I could secure my parents' favor and feel close to them was by being exceptional at everything I did and by taking care of them emotionally.

I became the "hero child" and offered emotional support to them because it felt like the only way to feel secure and close.

My emotional response

I felt isolated, lonely, abandoned, and even more unseen. I longed to be noticed and loved for who I was. I determined to make others happy and try to meet all their needs so that maybe then they would love me. I stuffed my negative emotions inside and tried not to cause any difficulty to anyone.

Beliefs I formed

Relational closeness is dependent on me keeping others happy. Any preferences, emotions, or actions that disappoint or displease others are dangerous because they threaten my security in a relationship. Love is something that is earned and I must perform (i.e., take care of the other person) to be loved. Essentially, I, as a unique person with my own desires, preferences, and ways of being, am not "worth it" to people who matter to me unless I am serving them and keeping them happy.

Vows I made

I will not be "weak." I will not disappoint others. I will not be a burden or high maintenance. I will not fail. I must keep others happy (or they will leave).

Strategies of relating

I learned to work hard to keep the people I love happy and ignore my own needs and feelings. I tried hard not to be "weak," unreasonable, or a burden. I denied parts of myself that didn't seem as pleasing to others. It felt like there wasn't room in the relationship for me.

As I grew older, I tended to become a "parent" in many relationships, particularly romantic relationships. I set aside my own needs and preferences if they were not pleasing to the other person or if it seemed like I might inconvenience them. It's still uncomfortable for me to express my needs and ask for help! I would force myself to "be loving" even if I didn't authentically feel it. This became very problematic in romantic relationships because I would end up not even existing in the relationship except as a caregiver to the other person. I believed unconsciously that it was somehow unkind, unreasonable, and dangerous to be disagreeable or express my feelings and desires if they bothered the other person.

Behaviors I engaged in due to my strategies of relating

I tended to hide what I really thought and felt (sometimes even from myself) if I thought the other person wouldn't like it or would be disappointed or inconvenienced. I would agree to do things just to keep the other person happy, not because I genuinely wanted to. I would take on too many tasks for myself and not ask for help or even refuse help because I didn't want to be a burden. I wouldn't allow myself to be vulnerable and express my needs because I feared the other person wouldn't have space for me and might not see me as "worth it."

How do others perceive me because of my behaviors?

People tended to perceive me as being agreeable and easygoing and would instinctively lean on me for support. Because I would so often refuse help and never ask for it, some people stopped offering help or asking me how I was doing. I was always "fine," and I think people in my life started to view me that way. I received feedback from a few close friends that I seemed intimidating sometimes, even though on the inside I felt vulnerable and just longing for love.

What is the truth?

The truth is I had created a ruling passion that I must have the love and approval of people who matter to me and feel relationally "close" to those I love in order to feel secure.

What does transformation look like?

It has been intensely freeing and humbling to look at this honestly and to acknowledge my ultimate pursuit in this area. It's such a subtle thing and hides so well, buried in many well-known and endorsed messages around loving, serving, and caring for others. And yet in this twisted form, it's interfered with me having healthy relationships. Transformation for me has looked like gradually peeling back layer after layer of how this shows up in my life, finding it and recognizing it in different relationships, interactions, and seasons of life. It's been challenging and humbling, but also beautiful to discover new compassion for myself, new honesty, and an experience of God's love of me that is life-changing. I can now see that I learned this strategy as a young child who tried to do her best and wanted to avoid being hurt again, but I don't have to keep on using that same strategy. What a profound relief to challenge these ways of being and thinking against the truth of what Jesus says about me and who I am. I'm starting to feel the freedom of enjoying relationships without the crippling fear of thinking it's all up to me to keep the relationship secure. I know that existing fully and honestly in a relationship is the pathway to deepest love, and if the other person leaves or doesn't like me, I'm still held in a love that will never leave me. I am finally relaxing into the space God has given me and enjoying being freely myself.

SHORT FORM ADDITIONAL EXAMPLE

Below is an example of using the questions to write a brief summary of the formation of your ruling passions. Although our lives are much more complex than a few short sentences, this can help give you a quick snapshot.

1. Shaping Experience: As a young girl, my father was critical of my looks; he never told me I was beautiful.
2. Emotion: I developed deep sadness. I felt ugly and undesirable.
3. Belief: I don't have what it takes on my own to be attractive. I am an ugly girl. I must be seductive and sexual to get men to love me and to give me feelings of value and worth.
4. Vow: I'll do whatever it takes to always appear attractive and win the heart of the man I'm after.
5. Strategy: I'll relate to men in a seductive manner that will get me the love I want.
6. Behavior: I become sexually seductive.
7. How Others Perceive Me: Others perceive me as carefree, flirtatious, suggestive. When they see me this way, it confirms my belief that I only have value as a sexual being. I then feel used and dirty.
8. Truth vs. False Belief: "I must be seductive and sexual to get men to love me and to give me feelings of value and worth" is exchanged for the truth that God loves me as I am without me having to be seductive. Getting involved sexually causes others to disrespect me, makes me feel worse, heightens my loneliness, and entraps me in a continuing cycle of sin, guilt, and self-loathing. I don't have to be seductive or sexual with men to feel loved or affirmed.

9. Transformation: I receive the love of God, obey God in all areas of my life, and be loved by and love others in appropriate, godly ways without being sexual.

ACKNOWLEDGMENTS

Writing a book is never a solo endeavor, despite the many long hours spent writing alone. There are many who have helped me along the way. I am full of gratitude to my colleagues and our wonderfully supportive team at ServingLeaders Ministries, who believed in this book despite my self-doubt. Laura Yoder, Joe Bruni, and Tucker Else endured my endless requests to discuss ideas, provided valuable input, made helpful revisions, and gave much-needed overall encouragement. Our always helpful and servant-hearted Cyndy Bergmaier readily aided me in dozens of ways—big and small—always with a cheerful smile. Heartfelt appreciation to pastors and dear friends Phil Carnuccio and Todd Madonna for your steadfast, faithful friendship. Langdon Palmer, our long walks and talks helped me immensely. Thank you, Kathryn James, Chip Roper, and Paige Britton, who reviewed early drafts of this manuscript. Thank you to my editors Ruth Castle, Barbara Juliani, Brandon Peterson, and the team at New Growth Press who skillfully and gently shepherded this neophyte through this arduous process.

I am forever grateful for the providential meeting with Sara Dormon when we "randomly" connected in a crowd of over one thousand people. Sara's encouragement was instrumental in motivating me to continue writing when I had given up and in helping me find my agent, D. J. Snell, who also doggedly and patiently encouraged me. I am indebted to the pastors who participated in our ServingLeaders' Pastoral Cohorts, ministry leader gatherings, and all the participants who have attended the Ruling Passions seminars on which this book is based. I have learned so much from you. Watching the light in your eyes brighten with understanding and hearing your testimonies of finding freedom from self-sabotage made my passion burn hotter for teaching and writing about the profound life-changing truths in this book.

Finally, Isaac, we walked closely together for decades. Your tender heart, passion for truth, loving friendship, and patient, wise, and persistent pursuit continue to influence me profoundly. Your pain, struggles, failures, and death were not in vain; they do not outweigh the eternal ways God has used you. God has brought beauty out of ashes. Soli Deo gloria.

NOTES

Introduction
1. This term is based on a sermon by Thomas Chalmers titled "The Expulsive Power of a New Affection."
2. Parker Palmer, "Leading from Within," *Insights on Leadership: Service, Stewardship, Spirit, and Servant-Leadership*, ed. Larry C. Spears (John Wiley, 1997), 202.

Chapter 1
1. John Piper, *The Pleasures of God* (Multnomah, 1991), 15, quoting Henry Scougal, *The Life of God in the Soul of Man* (Sprinkle Publications, 1986), 62.
2. Henry Scougal, *The Life of God in the Soul of Man* (Nichols and Noyes, 2006), 40.

Chapter 2
1. See Philip Ryken, *Galatians: Reformed Expository Commentary* (P&R Publishing, 2005), 55; John Stott, *The Message of Galatians* (InterVarsity Press, 1968), 49.
2. Stott, *The Message of Galatians*, 49–50.
3. Ryken, *Galatians*, 55.
4. Ryken, *Galatians*, 54.
5. Ryken, *Galatians*, 9.
6. Stott, *The Message of Galatians*, 51.
7. Stott, *The Message of Galatians*, 56–57.
8. John MacArthur, *The MacArthur New Testament Commentary: Galatians* (Moody Bible Institute, 1987), 50.
9. MacArthur, *The MacArthur New Testament Commentary: Galatians*, 51.
10. Stott, *The Message of Galatians*, 51; John MacArthur, *The MacArthur New Testament Commentary Galatians*, 51.
11. Moshe Halbertal and Avishai Margalit, *Idolatry* (Harvard University Press, 1992), 245–46.
12. Stott, *The Message of Galatians*, 52.

Chapter 3

1. Paul David Tripp, *Instruments in the Redeemer's Hands: People in Need of Change Helping People in Need of Change* (P&R Publishing, 2002), 66.
2. Timothy Keller, *Counterfeit Gods: The Empty Promises of Money, Sex, and Power, and the Only Hope that Matters* (Penguin, 2009), xvi–xviii.
3. Timothy Keller, "How to Talk About Sin in a Postmodern Age," *The Gospel Coalition* (blog), May 12, 2017, https://www.thegospelcoalition.org/article/how-to-talk-sin-in-postmodern-age/; see generally, Keller, *Counterfeit Gods*.
4. Moshe Halbertal and Avishai Margalit, *Idolatry* (Harvard University Press, 1992), 245–46.
5. John Calvin, *Institutes of Christian Religion* (I.11.8). John Calvin, Institutes of the Christian Religion, ed. John Thomas McNeill, trans. Ford Lewis Battles (Westminster John Knox Press, 1960), 1.11.8.
6. Keller, *Counterfeit Gods*, xvii.
7. Larry Crabb, *Understanding People: Why We Long for Relationship* (Zondervan, 1987), 153.
8. Crabb, *Understanding People*, 94, 111–13.
9. See, for example, C. S. Lewis, *Mere Christianity* (Macmillan, 1960), 120.
10. Keller, *Counterfeit Gods*, xvi–xviii.

Chapter 4

1. Diane M. Langberg, *Suffering and the Heart of God: How Trauma Destroys and Christ Restores* (New Growth Press, 2015), 198.
2. Diane M. Langberg, *Redeeming Power: Understanding Authority and Abuse in the Church* (Brazos Press, 2020), 35.
3. For a comprehensive discussion of the iceberg metaphor and its implications, see Larry Crabb, *Inside Out* (NavPress, 1988), 44–50; Crabb, *Understanding People*, 143.
4. Crabb, *Inside Out*, 44–45.

Chapter 6

1. Rebecca Manley Pippert, *Out of the Saltshaker and into the World*, 2nd ed. (InterVarsity Press, 1999), 53.
2. Timothy Keller, *Counterfeit Gods: The Empty Promises of Money, Sex, and Power, and the Only Hope that Matters* (Penguin, 2009), xviii.

3. Paul David Tripp, *Instruments in the Redeemer's Hands: People in Need of Change Helping People in Need of Change* (P&R Publishing, 2002), 69–70.

Chapter 7

1. Diane M. Langberg, *Redeeming Power Understanding Authority and Abuse in the Church* (Brazos Press, 2020), 127.

2. For an excellent discussion on the different types of power ministry leaders exercise, see Peter Scazzero, *The Emotionally Healthy Leader: How Transforming Your Inner Life Will Deeply Transform Your Church, Team, and the World* (Zondervan, 2015), 239–68.

3. Langberg, *Redeeming Power*, 35, quoting Howard Thurman, *Jesus and the Disinherited* (Beacon, 1976), 55.

Chapter 8

1. *Westminster Larger Catechism*, Q.1.

Chapter 9

1. See generally, Carl R. Trueman, *The Rise and Triumph of the Modern Self: Cultural Amnesia, Expressive Individualism, and the Road to Sexual Revolution* (Crossway, 2020).

2. Brian G. Hedges, "Saint Augustine on Rightly Ordered Love," *Brian G. Hedges* (blog), September 27, 2013, https://www.brianghedges.com/2013/09/saint-augustine-on-rightly-ordered-love.html.

3. Michael John Cusick, *Surfing for God: Discovering the Divine Desire beneath Sexual Struggle* (Thomas Nelson, 2012), 30–31; Larry Crabb, *Understanding People* (Zondervan, 1987), 107–19;

4. Joe Bruni, "Passion's Provocation and Purpose: Avoiding Idolatry in a World Ruled by Desire," *ServingLeaders* (blog), 2019, https://www.servingleaders.org/blog/2019/1/23/passions-provocation-and-purpose.

5. *Westminster Larger Catechism*, Q.1 (emphasis added).

6. Augustine, *Commentary on the Psalms,* Psalm 35.9, *New Advent*, retrieved from https://www.newadvent.org/fathers/1801035.htm.

7. Brian G. Hedges, "Saint Augustine on Rightly Ordered Love," *Brian G. Hedges* (blog), September 27, 2013, https://www.brianghedges.com/2013/09/saint-augustine-on-rightly-ordered-love.html.

8. C. S. Lewis, *Letters to Malcolm: Chiefly on Prayer* (Harcourt, 1992), 89–90.

9. Lewis, *Letters to Malcolm*, 89–90.

10. C. S. Lewis, *Mere Christianity* (Macmillan, 1960), 120 (emphasis added); see also Tish Harrison Warren, *Prayer in the Night: For Those Who Work or Watch or Weep* (InterVarsity Press, 2021), 223.

11. Lewis, *Mere Christianity*, 119.

12. Warren, *Prayer in the Night*, 223.

13. Lewis, *Mere Christianity*, 119.

14. C. S. Lewis, *The Weight of Glory* (MacMillan, 1949), 1.

15. Augustine, On Christian Doctrine, I.27-28, Translation from *Select Library of Nicene and Post-Nicene Fathers* https://faculty.georgetown.edu/jod/augustine/ddc1.html.

16. Timothy Keller, *God's Wisdom for Navigating Life: A Year of Daily Devotions in the Book of Proverbs* (Viking, 2017), 93.

17. Lewis, *Letters to Malcolm*, 89–90.

18. Brian Hedges, "Saint Augustine on Rightly Ordered Love," *Brian G. Hedges* (blog), September 27, 2013, https://www.brianghedges.com/2013/09/saint-augustine-on-rightly-ordered-love.html.

19. Augustine, *Confessions*, X.22. The Confessions, trans. Maria Boulding (Vintage Books, 1998).

Chapter 10

1. Philip Ryken, *Galatians: Reformed Expository Commentary* (P&R Publishing, 2005), 43.

2. John MacArthur, *The MacArthur New Testament Commentary: Galatians* (Moody Bible Institute, 1987), 42.

Chapter 11

1. I am indebted to Dr. Barbara Shaffer for this life-changing insight she shared in a personal communication form September 2001.

2. Scott Sauls, *From Weakness to Strength: 8 Vulnerabilities That Can Bring Out the Best in Your Leadership* (David C. Cook, 2017), 74.

3. Peter Scazzero, *The Emotionally Healthy Leader: How Transforming Your Inner Life Will Deeply Transform Your Church, Team, and the World* (Zondervan, 2015), 77.

4. Paul David Tripp, *Lead: 12 Gospel Principles for Leadership in the Church* (Crossway, 2020), 116.

5. David Powlison, *Safe and Sound: Standing Firm in Spiritual Battles* (New Growth Press, 2019), 17.

6. For a helpful discussion of strategies for engaging in spiritual warfare, see Tripp, *Lead*, 122–27.

Chapter 14

1. Dan Allender, *To Be Told: God Invites You to Coauthor Your Future* (Waterbrook Press, 2005), 76.
2. Dan Allender, *Healing the Wounded Heart: The Heartache of Sexual Abuse and the Hope of Transformation* (Baker Books, 2016), 45.
3. Allender, *Healing the Wounded Heart*, 45.
4. Dr. Kevin Huggins, lecture, Legal and Ethical Issues in Counseling, Cairn University (2001).
5. Henri Nouwen, *The Living Reminder: Service and Prayer in Memory of Jesus Christ*, 3rd ed. (HarperOne, 2009), 20–21.
6. Richard Plass and James Cofield, *The Relational Soul: Moving from False Self to Deep Connection* (InterVarsity Press, 2014), 51.
7. Abraham Joshua Heschel, *Moral Grandeur and Spiritual Audacity*, ed. Susanna Heschel (Farrar, Straus and Giroux, 1997), 334.
8. Nouwen, *The Living Reminder*, 22.
9. Dr. Kevin Huggins, lecture, Legal and Ethical Issues in Counseling, Cairn University (2001).
10. Developed and adapted from Dr. Kevin Huggins, lecture, Legal and Ethical Issues in Counseling, Cairn University (2001).
11. Dr. Kevin Huggins, lecture, Legal and Ethical Issues in Counseling, Cairn University (2001).
12. There are many situations where it is not appropriate or safe to re-expose oneself to painful situations, and wisdom dictates not doing so (e.g., reconnecting with an abuser, revisiting places of drug addiction or high crime areas).

Chapter 15

1. Peter Scazzero, *The Emotionally Healthy Leader: How Transforming Your Inner Life Will Deeply Transform Your Church, Team, and the World* (Zondervan, 2015), 72–75.
2. Peter Scazzero, *Emotionally Healthy Spirituality: It's Impossible to Be Spiritually Mature While Remaining Emotionally Immature*, updated ed. (Zondervan, 2017), 24.
3. Dan Allender and Tremper Longman III, *The Cry of the Soul: How Our Emotions Reveal Our Deepest Questions about God* (NavPress, 1994), 24–25.
4. Scazzero, *Emotionally Healthy Spirituality*, 24–25.
5. The term "spiritual bypassing" was coined by psychologist John Welwood, *Toward a Psychology of Awakening: Buddhism,*

Psychotherapy and the Path of Personal and Spiritual Transformation (Shambhala Publications, 2000).

6. Scazzero, *Emotionally Healthy Spirituality*, 45–46.

7. Wayne Grudem, *Systematic Theology: An Introduction to Biblical Doctrine* (Zondervan Academic, 1994), 446–47; Bill and Kristi Gaultiere, *Healthy Feelings, Thriving Faith: Growing Emotionally and Spiritually through the Enneagram* (Revell, 2023), 256. For an informative discussion on how human beings are made in the image of God as personal, rational, emotional, and volitional beings, see Larry Crabb, *Understanding People: Why We Long for Relationship* (Zondervan, 1987), 86–160. For a helpful and detailed discussion on the importance of emotions, see Scazzero, *Emotionally Healthy Spirituality*; Peter Scazzero, *The Emotionally Healthy Church* (Zondervan, 2003).

8. Bill and Kristi Gaultiere, *Healthy Feelings, Thriving Faith*, 13.

9. Timothy Keller, *Walking with God through Pain and Suffering* (Penguin, 2013), 242.

10. For more on this, see, for example, Peter Scazzero, *Emotionally Healthy Spirituality*; Peter Scazzero, *Emotionally Healthy Church*.

11. Judith Herman, *Trauma and Recovery: The Aftermath of Violence—from Domestic Abuse to Political Terror* (Basic Books, 2015), 176.

12. Herman, *Trauma and Recovery*, 133–34.

13. Bessel van der Kolk, *The Body Keeps the Score: Brain, Mind, and Body in the Healing of Trauma* (Penguin, 2014), 53, 64; Dan Allender, *Healing the Wounded Heart* (Baker Books, (2016), 49–69; Stephen Porges, "Polyvagal Theory: A Science of Safety," *Frontiers in Integrative Neuroscience* 16:871227 (May 2022), https://doi.org/10.3389/fnint.2022.871227; Louis Cozolino, *The Neuroscience of Psychotherapy: Healing the Social Brain (Norton Series on Interpersonal Neurobiology)* Third Edition, (W.W. Norton & Company, 2017).

14. Van der Kolk, *The Body Keeps the Score*, 80.

15. Van der Kolk, *The Body Keeps the Score*, 80.

16. I am indebted to Diane Langberg for this insight she shared in a personal communication form September 2007.

17. Cornelius Plantinga, Jr., *Not the Way It's Supposed to Be: A Breviary of Sin* (Eerdmans, 1996), 131.

18. *Imago Hearts*, Newsletter (January 17, 2024); Allender, *Healing the Wounded Heart*, 45.

19. Allender, *Healing the Wounded Heart*, 144. See also, Gregory L. Jantz, *Healing the Scars of Childhood Abuse: Moving beyond the Past into a Healthy Future* (Revell, 2017), 159.

20. Bill and Kristi Gaultiere, *Healthy Feelings, Thriving Faith*, 256.

21. Curt Thompson, *The Deepest Place: Suffering and the Formation of Hope* (Zondervan, 2023), 127.

22. Brennan Manning, *A Glimpse of Jesus: The Stranger to Self-Hatred* (Dimension Books, 1982), 33–34.

23. William Struthers, *Wired for Intimacy: How Pornography Hijacks the Male Brain* (InterVarsity Press, 2009), 99–106.

24. Michael John Cusick, *Surfing for God: Discovering the Divine Desire beneath Sexual Struggle* (Thomas Nelson, 2012), 14.

25. Crabb, *Understanding People*, 164.

Chapter 16

1. Jimmy Dodd, *Survive or Thrive: 6 Relationships Every Pastor Needs* (David C. Cook, 2015), 113.

Chapter 17

1. A. W. Tozer, *The Knowledge of the Holy* (HarperCollins, 1978), 1.

2. Timothy R. Jennings, *The God-Shaped Brain: How Changing Your View of God Transforms Your Life*, expanded ed. (InterVarsity Press, 2017), 56.

3. Judith Beck, *Cognitive Behavioral Therapy: Basics and Beyond* (The Guilford Press, 2011), 32–33. For more on this topic, see Jeffrey Young, *Cognitive Therapy for Personality Disorders: A Schema-Focused Approach* (Professional Resource Press, 1999).

4. Jennings, *The God-Shaped Brain*, 34–36.

5. Larry Crabb, *Understanding People: Why We Long for Relationship* (Zondervan, 1987), 131; Judith Herman, *Trauma and Recovery: The Aftermath of Violence—from Domestic Abuse to Political Terror* (Basic Books, 2015), 178.

6. Jennings, *The God-Shaped Brain*, 57.

7. Dr. Kevin Huggins, lecture, Legal and Ethical Issues in Counseling, Cairn University (2001).

8. A helpful resource for deeper study of this crucial topic can be found in Timothy Keller, *Walking with God through Pain and Suffering* (Penguin, 2013).

9. Keller, *Walking with God through Pain and Suffering*, 260.

10. Joni Eareckson Tada, "Ten Words That Changed Everything About My Suffering," *Desiring God* (blog), September 7, 2021, https://www.desiringgod.org/articles/ten-words-that-changed-everything-about-my-suffering.

11. Joni Eareckson Tada, "God Permits What He Hates," *Joni and Friends* (blog), May 15, 2023, https://web.archive.org/web/20150621063852/http://www.joniandfriends.org/radio/5-minute/god-permits-what-he-hates1; for the story of Eareckson's life, see also, Joni Eareckson Tada, *The God I Love: A Lifetime of Walking with Jesus* (Zondervan, 2003).

12. Timothy Keller, *The Songs of Jesus: A Year of Daily Devotionals in the Psalms* (Viking, 2015), 81, quoting Derek Kidner, *Psalms 1-72: An Introduction and Commentary* (InterVarsity Press, 2014) (emphasis added).

13. Curt Thompson, *The Deepest Place: Suffering and the Formation of Hope* (Zondervan, 2023), 93.

Chapter 18

1. Dan Allender, *Leading with a Limp: Turning Your Struggles into Strengths* (WaterBrook Press, 2006), 161. For a helpful resource in writing your story, see Adam Young, *Make Sense of Your Story: Why Engaging Your Past with Kindness Changes Everything* (Baker Books, 2024).

2. Dan Allender, *To Be Told: God Invites You to Coauthor Your Future* (Waterbrook Press, 2005), 10 (emphasis added).

3. Dan Allender, *Healing the Wounded Heart: The Heartache of Sexual Abuse and the Hope of Transformation* (Baker Books, 2016), 45–46.

4. Great resources to help you understand the importance exploring your family of origin can be found in Peter Scazzero, *Emotionally Healthy Spirituality: It's Impossible to Be Spiritually Mature While Remaining Emotionally Immature*, updated ed. (Zondervan, 2017), 71; Peter Scazzero, *Emotionally Healthy Discipleship: Moving from Shallow Christianity to Deep Transformation* (Zondervan, 2021), 164–71.

5. Scazzero, *Emotionally Healthy Spirituality*, 71–77; Scazzero, *Emotionally Healthy Discipleship*, 173.

6. For a list of insightful questions, see Scazzero, *Emotionally Healthy Discipleship*, 171.

7. For a comprehensive list of positive beliefs rooted in Scripture, see Sue Corl, *Shaking off the Shackles: Live Out Your Divine Birthright and Thrive Like Never Before* (Morgan Pierce Media & Publishing, 2024), 151–56.

8. Larry Crabb, *Inside Out* (NavPress, 1988), 119.

Chapter 19

1. Peter Scazzero, *Emotionally Healthy Spirituality: It's Impossible to Be Spiritually Mature While Remaining Emotionally Immature*, updated ed. (Zondervan, 2017), 19.